HATHA

THE REPORT OF A PERS

By Theos Bernard, M.A., Ph.D., LL.B.

By the same author:

Heaven Lies Within Us
Hindu Philosophy - Philosophical Foundations of India
Land of a Thousand Buddhas

First published in the UK: 1950
This edition: 2007
Printed and bound in Korea
ISBN 978-0-9552412-2-2

Harmony Publishing
25 Rodney Street
Edinburgh
EH7 4EL
Scotland
www.harmonypublishing.org
contact@harmonypublishing.org

To Ganna Walska

This account of the death of the author was related by Mr. G. A. Bernard, the author's father:

"In 1947, Theos Bernard was on a mission to the KI monastery in western Tibet in search of some special manuscripts. While on his way, rioting broke out among the Hindus and the Moslems in that section of the hills; all Moslems including women and children in the little village from which Theos departed were killed.

"The Hindus then proceeded into the mountains in pursuit of the Moslems who had accompanied Theos as guides and muleteers. These Moslems, it is reported, learning of the killings, escaped, leaving Theos and his Tibetan boy alone on the trail. It is further reported that both were shot and their bodies thrown into the river.

"To date we have not been able to get any authentic information on the entire circumstances of his death, nor have we any line on the effects Theos had with him. That region of Tibet is so very remote that it is unlikely we shall ever learn the full details."

§

C o n t e n t s

PREFACE

THIS STUDY is the report of a Westerner who has practised Yoga under a teacher in India. The primary purpose of the investigation was to test by personal experience the techniques of Hatha Yoga. For this purpose I went to India and Tibet. First I made a general acquaintance with India, meeting and talking with people from every walk of life, rajas to beggars, kavirajas to magicians, scholars to students, saints to sadhus. I visited colleges, libraries, museums, temples, shrines, ashramas and ghats from Calcutta to Bombay, from Kashmir to Ceylon, including all the outstanding cities, such as Allahabad, Benares, Agra, Delhi, Lahore, Srinagar, Peshwar, Uddipur, Hyderabad, Mysore, Bangalore, Madras, Madura, and Trichinopoly. This alone consumed several months, but provided an impression of India's culture to be had in no other way.

After the 'grand tour' I submitted to a course of traditional training in Hatha Yoga, taking notes and making critical observations in order to appraise the results in the light of experience rather than of theory. I was, in fact, induced to make this practical trial of Yoga because of the disappointments I experienced in connection with Yoga theory. The theories, about which there is an abundant literature, were confusing rather than informative regarding the practical content and discipline of Hatha Yoga. To this end I became the sincere disciple of a highly esteemed teacher and settled down at his retreat in the hills near Ranchi. Under his supervision and guidance I adhered to the rigid discipline imposed upon one who wishes to practise Hatha Yoga.

In order to further my studies, it was suggested by my teacher that I go to Tibet. According to him, what has become mere tradition in India is still living and visible in the ancient monasteries of that isolated land of mysteries. Immediately I set forth. My first intimate contact with the training as it is found in Tibet was through a renowned hermit on the Tibetan border in northern Sikkim. With him, by means of an interpreter, I was able to converse about the doctrines and literature of Tibetan Lamaism. Through him I was able to make a general inventory of the literature of the Kargyüpa sect, which contains the earliest material taken into Tibet from India from the seventh to the eleventh century. My travels culminated in a pilgrimage to the holy city, Lhasa, where I was accepted as an incarnation of a Tibetan saint. This removed all obstacles and enabled me to take part in the religious ceremonies of the Jo-Wo Kang and the Ramoche, the two sacred temples in Lhasa, in rites held at the tomb of the last Dalai Lama in the Nam Gyal Ch'oide of the Potala, as well as to attend the services held in many of the smaller shrines of that great palace. Opportunity was given for me to participate in ceremonies and discuss the teachings with some of the leading lamas of the famed monasteries of Drepong, Sera, Ganden, Dochen, Dra-Yarpa, Palk'or Ch'oide, at Gyantse, Tashi-Lumpo, in Shigatse, and Saskya, 'the Oxford of Asia', which was the original seat of learning in Tibet and today houses one of the largest libraries of the land.

During my stay in Lhasa, a learned geshe from the Sera monastery lived with me. He helped me to find and classify the literature I sought and instructed me as well in the religious practices used in the monasteries of the Gelupa sect, the ruling sect today. At the same time I was able to have the guidance of another lama, who was the head of a small Kargyüpa monastery a few days distant from Lhasa. He was with me daily for some time, and we discussed Kargyüpa beliefs and practices as contrasted with those of other sects. Throughout my entire stay in Tibet I was constantly in touch with other lamas of good repute, checking what I had heard and read. A survey of this sort could only scratch the surface, but it helped me to interpret my practical discipline and to obtain a sense of what Yoga means in their lives. I do not report my Tibetan experience here, because it was merely background for my training in India.

Any attempt to prove the merits of the 'art of Yoga' would be futile. If a thousand volumes were quoted in its favour and all the rules of logic and sophistry were employed, the doubts and scepticism of modern man would still remain. Therefore this study is not an attempt to prove the merits of Yoga or to explain its results. Instead, I here present a report of my personal experiences in learning and practising the basic techniques of Hatha Yoga, in order to give the Western reader an accurate account of the conduct of a typical oriental course in that Yoga; and I accompany my description with references to the relevant passages from the classic texts in order that the critical reader may estimate the extent to which tradition is followed and may more readily correlate theory and practice. The chief texts I have used for this purpose are, for obvious reasons, the most familiar translations: *Hatha Yoga Pradipika*, translated by Pancham Sinh; *Gheranda Samhita*, translated by Sris Chandra Vasu; *Siva Samhita*, translated by Rai Bahadur Srisa Chandra Vidyarnava. Where there seemed to be a questionable interpretation of the text I have taken the liberty, for the sake of consistency, to make a few minor corrections.

When I went to India, I did not present myself as an academic research student, trying to probe into the intimacies of ancient cultural patterns; instead, I became a disciple and in this way one of the Yogis in body and spirit, without reservation, for I wanted to 'taste' their teachings.[1] This required that I take part in many religious ceremonies, for everything in India is steeped in the formalities of rites and rituals. However, such forms theoretically are not recognized as an essential factor in the practice of Hatha Yoga.

Success cannot be attained by adopting a particular dress (Vesa). It cannot be gained by telling tales. Practice alone is the means to success. This is true, there is no doubt. Asanas (postures), various kumbhakas (breathing techniques), and other divine means, all should be practised in the practice of Hatha Yoga, till the fruit

---

1) The relation of guru and disciple is discussed in Siva Samhita, iii, 10–19: "Now I shall tell you how easily to attain success in Yoga, by knowing which the Yogis never fail in the practice of Yoga. Only the knowledge imparted by a Guru, through his lips is powerful and useful; otherwise it becomes fruitless, weak and very painful. He who is devoted to any knowledge, while pleasing his Guru with every attention, readily obtains the fruits of that knowledge. There is not the least doubt that Guru is father, Guru is mother, and Guru is God even; and as such he should be served by all with their thought, word and deed. By Guru's favour everything good relating to one's self is obtained. So the Guru ought to be daily served; else there can be nothing auspicious. Let him salute his Guru after walking three times round him, and touching with his right hand his lotus feet.

"The person who has control over himself attains verily success through faith; none other can succeed. Therefore, with faith, Yoga should be practised with care and perseverance. Those who are addicted to sensual pleasures or keep bad company, who are disbelievers, who are devoid of respect towards their Guru, who resort to promiscuous assemblies, who are addicted to false and vain controversies, who are cruel in their speech, and who do not give satisfaction to their Guru never attain success. The first condition of success is the firm belief that it (vidya) must succeed and be fruitful; the second condition is having faith in it; the third is respect towards the Guru; the fourth is the spirit of Universal equality; the fifth is the restraint of the organs of sense; the sixth is moderate eating, these are all. There is no seventh condition. Having received instructions in Yoga, and obtained a Guru who knows Yoga, let him practise with earnestness and faith, according to the method taught by the teacher."

— Raja Yoga — is obtained.[2]

However, in order to learn I submitted myself completely to the traditional customs of each teacher, for I was anxious to learn everything that would contribute to a fuller understanding of Yoga.

My principal literary guide has been Hatha *Yoga Pradipika*; hence I shall adopt its sequence in relating my personal experiences in learning and practising these techniques. In order that this study may be self-contained and that the reader shall not be burdened to search elsewhere for the other texts, which are extremely difficult to obtain, I quote at length from all of them. This will show how much they are in accord and at the same time will acquaint the student with the style of Hatha Yoga literature. When comments can contribute to an understanding of the question under consideration, I make them briefly; if, on the other hand, obscure statements are not of immediate concern, I disregard them. Many strange statements concerning the supernatural and the miraculous become clearer as the student progresses in his studies; it is best to ignore those which do not relate to the practice of Hatha Yoga.

As far as it is possible to do so by still photography, the various postures and disciplines which I have learned are illustrated by the thirty-six photographs appended. These are for the most part asanas; a few mudras are shown. The most elementary postures are omitted, not needing illustration. It is obviously impossible to show adequately by such photographs the performance of purification practices and breathing exercises. The photographs of the author here included were recently taken. The plates are arranged and numbered in the order in which the postures are treated in the text, with a few exceptions, which are referred to only in the footnotes. These photographs can be compared with the eighty-seven lithographs in Richard Schmidt's *Fakire und Fakirtum im alten und modernen Indien*, which illustrate the same postures and in addition some of the most elementary postures, which I have not included. More recently there have appeared other illustrations of the postures, notably those in Kuvalayananda's *Asanas*.

To my teachers of India and Tibet, who, shunning public acclaim, must perforce remain anonymous, I am deeply indebted. Thanks are

---

2) *Hatha Yoga Pradipika*, i, 68–69.

due to Professor Herbert W. Schneider, for his constant encouragement and helpful suggestions in the preparation of the manuscript, and to Professor Henry Zimmer, for his valuable guidance and technical assistance.

THEOS BERNARD

INTRODUCTION

HATHA YOGA is a discipline involving various bodily and mental controls,[1] but central to them all is the regulation of the breath. Hatha is derived from two roots, 'ha' (sun) and 'tha' (moon), which symbolically refer to the flowing of breath in the right nostril, called the 'sun breath', and the flowing of breath in the left nostril, called the 'moon breath'. Yoga is derived from the root 'yuj' (to join); therefore, Hatha Yoga is the uniting of these two breaths. The effect is believed to induce a mental condition called samadhi. This is not an imaginary or mythical state, though it is explained by myths, but is an actual condition that can be subjectively experienced and objectively observed.

In order to bring about a stabilization of the breath, considerable emphasis is placed upon purification of the body and the use of various physical techniques. The training of the physical body as an end in itself is called Ghatastha Yoga. It is maintained that the methods employed do not violate any of the physical laws of the body; so they have been given the name Physiological Yoga. The practices are said to make dynamic a latent force in the body called Kundalini; hence the term Kundalini Yoga is frequently employed. All processes utilized are directed toward the single aim of stilling the mind. For this condition the method applied is known as Laya Yoga. The complete subjugation of the mind is considered to be the Royal Road and is called Raja Yoga. All these forms are often classified under the general heading Tantrik Yoga, since they represent the practical discipline based on Tantrik philosophy;[2] but 'tantra' is used loosely for a variety of systems, chiefly

---

1) The traditional meaning of the word Hatha is: (1) violence, force; (2) oppression, rapine; it is used adverbially in the sense of 'forcibly', 'violently', 'suddenly', 'against one's will'; hence this form of Yoga is sometimes called 'forced Yoga'.

2) See the works of Sir John Woodroffe, who also wrote under the pseudonym Arthur Avalon: *The Serpent Power, Shakti and Shakta, Garland of Letters, The Great Liberation*, and *Principles of Tantra* (in two volumes). The chief classic texts are now available in English. Among the important earlier treatments of our subject should be mentioned Oman's *The Mystics, Ascetics, and Saints of India*, and Schmidt's *Fakire und Fakirtum im alten und modernen Indien*. Schmidt's work is based largely on Oman's but contains a German translation of the *Gheranda Samhita* and a valuable series of il-

for the purpose of distinguishing them from other forms of non-physiological discipline. These other forms of Yoga offer intellectual and devotional processes for subduing the mind and producing tranquillity, but do not prescribe any system of physiological or bodily discipline.[3]

The techniques of Hatha Yoga are given in the classic texts: *Hatha Yoga Pradipika*, *Gheranda Samhita* and *Siva Samhita*. These are the leading treatises on the subject. The first is considered to be the standard authority, and in many instances the verses of the second correspond closely. The third presents a fuller account and introduces a brief outline of the general attitude toward Hatha Yoga, showing its importance and metaphysical foundation.[4] The other texts assume that

lustrations collected in India by Garbe in 1886. The more recent works and editions are noted in the Bibliography. The two volumes by Kuvalayananda contain illustrations of most of the postures.

3) The generally accepted forms of Yoga are discussed in *Siva Samhita*, v, 9: "The Yoga is of four kinds: —First Mantra-Yoga, second Hatha-Yoga, third Laya-Yoga, fourth Raja-Yoga, which discards duality." Evans-Wentz, in *Tibetan Yoga and Secret Doctrines*, p. 33, says: "The various aspects or parts of Yoga and their general relationship to one another may now be set forth concisely by the following table:

GIVING

"THE PART	MASTER OF	AND LEADING TO YOGIC CONTROL OF
I. Hatha Yoga	breath	physical body and vitality.
II. Laya Yoga	will	powers of mind.
(1) Bhakti Yoga	love	powers of divine love.
(2) Shakti Yoga	energy	energizing forces of Nature.
(3) Mantra Yoga	sound	powers of sound vibration.
(4) Yantra Yoga	form	powers of geometrical form.
III. Dhyana Yoga	thought	powers of though-processes.
IV. Raja Yoga	method	powers of discrimination.
(1) Jnana Yoga	knowledge	powers of intellect.
(2) Karma Yoga	activity	powers of action.
(3) Kundalini Yoga	Kundalini	powers of psychic-nerve force.
(4) Samadhi Yoga	self	powers of ecstasy."

4) *Siva Samhita*, i, 1–19, opens with the following discussion, "The Jnana [Gnosis] alone is eternal; it is without beginning or end; there exists no other real substance. Diversities which we see in the world are results of sense-conditions; when the latter cease, then this Jnana alone, and nothing else, remains. I, Isvara, the lover of my devotees, and Giver of spiritual emancipation to all creatures, thus declare the science of Yoganusasana (the exposition of Yoga). In it are discarded all those doctrines of disputants, which lead to false knowledge. It is for the spiritual disenthralment of persons whose minds are undistracted and fully turned towards me.

"Some praise truth, others purification and asceticism; some praise forgiveness, others equal-the student is thoroughly familiar with these principles. None of them discuss Yoga, for they were meant to be outlines, and the details were supposed to be supplied by the teacher. Yoga was never intended to serve as a 'spiritual correspondence course', but was given as a method of 'self-culture' to be practised under supervision. It was never intended that Yoga should be practised without the guidance of a teacher. It is just as impossible to do so as it is to become a finished musician from a mail-order course. The texts were meant only to serve as a guide; a teacher was to furnish the details necessary in each individual case. All the texts are couched in the 'mysterious', or technical, phraseology of tantrik literature which presents such a stumbling block for the western mind.

The texts agree that Hatha Yoga is the stepping stone and that ultimate liberation comes from the practice of Raja Yoga. The Pradipika opens:

Salvation to Adinatha (Siva) who expounded the knowledge of Hatha Yoga, which like a staircase leads the aspirant to the high-pinnacled Raja Yoga. Yogin

---

ity and sincerity. Some praise alms-giving, others laud sacrifices made in honour of one's ancestors; some praise action (Karma), others think dispassion (Vairagya) to be the best. Some wise persons praise the performance of the duties of the householder; other authorities hold up fire-sacrifice, &c., as the highest. Some praise Mantra Yoga, others the frequenting of places of pilgrimage. Thus diverse are the ways which people declare for emancipation. Being thus diversely engaged in this world, even those who still know what actions are good and what evil, though free from sin, become subject to bewilderment. Persons who follow these doctrines, having committed good and bad actions, constantly wander in the worlds, in the cycle of births and deaths, bound by dire necessity. Others, wiser among the many, and eagerly devoted to the investigation of the occult, declare that the souls are many and eternal, and omnipresent. Others say, 'Only those things can be said to exist which are perceived through the senses and nothing besides them; where is heaven or hell?' Such is their firm belief. Others believe the world to be a current of consciousness and no material entity; some call the void as the greatest. Others believe in two essences: Matter (Prakriti) and Spirit (Purusa). Thus believing in widely different doctrines, with faces turned away from the supreme goal, think, according to their understanding and education, that this universe is without God; others believe there is God, basing their assertions on various irrefutable arguments, founded on texts, declaring difference between soul and God, and anxious to establish the existence of God. These and many other sages with various different denominations, have been declared in the Sastras as leaders of the human mind into delusions. It is not possible to describe fully the doctrines of these persons so fond of quarrel and contention; people thus wander in this universe, being driven away from the path of emancipation.

"Having studied all the Sastras and having pondered over them well, again and again, this Yoga Sastras has been found to be the only true and firm doctrine. Since by Yoga all this verily is known as a certainty, all exertion should be made to acquire it. What is the necessity then of any other doctrines? This Yoga Sastras, now being declared by us, is a very secret doctrine, only to be revealed to a high souled pious devotee throughout the three worlds."

Svatmarama, after saluting his Guru Srinatha, explains Hatha Yoga solely for the attainment of Raja Yoga. Owing to the darkness arising from the multiplicity of opinions which spring from error people are unable to know the Raja Yoga. Compassionate Svatmarama holds the Hatha Yoga Pradipika like a torch to dispel it.[5]

Some of the most highly esteemed teachers of ancient India maintain that they have received enlightenment through the practices of Hatha Yoga and according to tradition passed the method down by word of mouth, from teacher to pupil, to the present day.

Matsyendra, Goraksa,[6] etc., knew Hatha Vidya and by their favour Yogin Svatmarama also knows it. (The following Siddhas [masters] are said to have existed in former times:—) Sri Adinatha (Siva), Matsyendra, Sabara, Ananada, Bhairava, Chaurangi, Minanatha, Goraksanatha, Virupaksa, Bilesaya, Manthana, Bhairava. Siddhi, Buddha, Kanthadi, Korantaka, Surananda, Siddhapada, Charpati, Kaneri, Pujyanada, Nityanatha, Niranjana, Kapali, Vindunatha, Kaka-Chandisvara, Allama, Prabhudeva, Ghoda, Choli, Tintini, Bhanuki, Naradeva, Khanda, Kapalika. These and other Mahasiddhas (great masters), through the potency of Hatha Yoga, breaking the sceptre of death, are roaming in the universe. Like a house protecting one from the heat of the sun, Hatha Yoga shelters all suffering from Tapas; and, similarly, it is the supporting tortoise, as it were, for those who are constantly devoted to the practice of Yoga.[7]

---

5) *Hatha Yoga Pradipika*, i, 1–3. Compare *Gheranda Samhita*, opening verse, "I salute that Adisvara who taught first the science of Hatha Yoga—a science that stands out as a ladder that leads to the higher heights of Raja Yoga."

6) For the life and teachings see Briggs, *Gorakhnath and the Kanphata Yogis*. See also Mitra, *Yoga Vasishtha Maharamayana of Valmiki*, and Evants-Wentz, *Tibet's Great Yogi Milarepa*.

7) For biographical accounts of two other renowned Yogis see *Hatha Yoga Pradipika*, i. 4–10. Compare the opening discussion in *Gheranda Samhita*, i, 1–11: "Once Canda-Kapali went to the hermitage of Gheranda, saluted him with great reverence and devotion, and inquired of him. 'O Master of Yoga! O best of the Yogins! O Lord! I wish now to hear the physiological Yoga, which leads to the knowledge of truth (or Tattva-Jnana).' 'Well asked, indeed, O mighty armed! I shall tell thee, O child! what thou askest me. Attend to it with diligence. There are no fetters like those of illusion (Maya), no strength like that which comes from discipline (Yoga), there is no friend higher than knowledge (Jnana), and no greater enemy than Egoism (Ahamkara). As by learning the alphabets one can, through practice, master all the sciences, so by thoroughly practising first the (physical) training, one acquires the Knowledge of the True. On account of good and bad deeds, the bodies of all animated beings are produced, and the bodies give rise to work (Karma which leads to rebirth) and thus the circle is continued like that of a rotating mill. As the rotating mill in drawing water from a well goes up and down, moved by the bullocks filling and exhausting the buckets again and again), so the soul passes through life and death moved by its Deeds. Like unto an unbaked earthen pot thrown in water, the body is soon decayed (in this world). Bake it hard in the fire of Yoga in order

Hatha Yoga is not taught indiscriminately to everyone, for it is be-lieved that "a yogi, desirous of success, should keep the knowledge of Hatha Yoga secret; for it becomes potent by concealing, and impotent by exposing."[8]

In order to become worthy of the teachings, the student must first fulfil the moral requirements called the yamas and niyamas, which are the moral prerequisites to the study of Yoga.

The ten Yamas (rules of conduct) are: ahimsa (non-injuring), truth, non-stealing, continence, forgiveness, endurance, compassion, sincerity, sparing diet and clean-liness. The ten Niyamas (rules of inner control) mentioned by those proficient in the knowledge of Yoga are: Tapas (penance), contentment, belief in God, charity, adoration of God, hearing discourses on the principles of religion, modesty, intel-lect, meditation, and Yajna [sacrifice].[9]

---

to strengthen and purify the body.

"The seven exercises which appertain to this Yoga of the body are the following: Purifica-tion, strengthening, steadying, calming, and those leading to lightness, perception, and isolation. 1st—The purification is acquired by the regular performance of six practices (purification processes); 2nd—Asana or posture gives Drdhata or strength; 3rd—Mudra gives Sthirata or steadiness; 4th—Pratyahara gives Dhirata or calmness; 5th—Pranayama gives lightness or Laghiman; 6th—Dhyana gives perception (Pratyaksatva) of Self; and 7th—Samadhi gives isolation (Nirliptata), which is verily the Freedom."

8) *Hatha Yoga Pradipika*, i, II.

9) *ibid.,* 17–18. Requirements for different forms of Yoga are discussed in *Siva Samhita*, v, 10–14: "Know that aspirants are of four orders:—mild, moderate, ardent and the most ardent—the best who can cross the ocean of the world.

"(Mild) entitled to Mantra-Yoga. Men of small enterprise, oblivious, sickly and finding faults with their teachers; avaricious sinful gourmands, and attached helplessly to their wives; fickle, timid, diseased, not independent, and cruel; those whose characters are bad and who are weak—know all the above to be mild sadhaks. With great efforts such men succeed in twelve years; them the teacher should know fit for the Mantra-Yoga.

"(Moderate) entitled to Laya-Yoga. Liberal-minded, merciful, desirous of virtue, sweet in their speech; who never go to extremes in any undertaking—these are the middling. These are to be initiated by the teacher in Laya-Yoga.

"(Ardent) entitled to Hatha Yoga. Steady-minded, knowing the Laya-Yoga, independent, full of energy, magnanimous, full of sympathy, forgiving, truthful, courageous, full of faith, worshippers of the lotus-feet of their Gurus, engaged always in the practice of Yoga—know such men to be adhimatra. They obtain success in the practice of Yoga within six years, and ought to be initiated in Hatha Yoga and its branches.

"(The most ardent) entitled to all Yogas. Those who have the largest amount of energy, are en-terprising, engaging, heroic, who know the sastras, and are persevering, free from the effects of blind emotions, and not easily confused, who are in the prime of their youth, moderate in their diet, rulers of their senses, fearless, clean, skilful, charitable, a help to all; competent, firm, talented, contented, forgiving, good-natured, religious, who keep their endeavours secret, of sweet speech, peaceful, who have faith in scriptures and are worshippers of God and Guru, who are averse to fritter away

The text goes a step further and outlines the forms of conduct that hinder one's progress and those that enable him to succeed.

Yoga is destroyed by the following six causes: —Overeating, exertion, talkativeness, adhering to rules (i.e. cold bath in the morning, eating at night, eating fruits only), company of men, and unsteadiness. The following six bring speedy success in Yoga:—courage, daring, perseverance, discriminative knowledge, faith, aloofness from company.[10]

These general restrictions and recommendations apply to all forms of Yoga.

---

their time in society, and are free from any grievous malady, who are acquainted with the duties of the adhimatra, and are the practitioners of every kind of Yoga—undoubtedly, they obtain success in three years; they are entitled to be initiated in all kinds of Yoga, without any hesitation."

10) *Hatha Yoga Pradipika*. i, 15–16. Compare the discussion of obstacles given in Siva Samhita, v, 1–8: "Parvati said, 'O Lord, O beloved Sankara! tell me, for the sake of those whose minds search after the supreme end, the obstacles and the hindrances to Yoga.' Siva said, 'Hear, O Goddess! I shall tell thee all the obstacles that stand in the path of yoga. For the attainment of emancipation enjoyments (Bhoga) are the greatest of all impediments.

" 'BHOGA (enjoyment). Women, beds, seats, dresses, and riches are obstacles to Yoga. Betels, dainty dishes, carriages, kingdoms, lordliness and powers; gold, silver, as well as copper, gems, wood, and kine; learning the Vedas and the Sastras; dancing, singing and ornaments; harp, flute and drum; riding on elephants and horses; wives and children, worldly enjoyments; all these arc so many impediments. These are the obstacles which arise from bhoga (enjoyment). Hear now the impediments which arise from ritualistic religion.

" 'DHARMA (Ritualism of Religion). The following are the obstacles which dharma interposes:—ablutions, worship of deities, observing the sacred days of the moon, fire, sacrifice, hankering after Moksa, vows and penances, fasts, religious observances, silence, the ascetic practices, contemplation and the object of contemplation, Mantras, and alms-giving, worldwide fame, excavating and endowing of tanks, wells, ponds, convents and groves; sacrifices, vows of starvation, Chandrayana, and pilgrimages.

" 'JNANA (Knowledge-obstacles). Now I shall describe, O Parvati, the obstacles which arise from knowledge. Sitting in the Gomukha posture and practising Dhauti (washing the intestines by Hatha Yoga). Knowledge of the distribution of the Nadis (the vessels of the human body), learning of pratyahara (subjugation of senses), trying to awaken the Kundalini force, by moving quickly the belly (a process of Hatha Yoga), entering into the path of the Indriyas, and knowledge of the action of the Nadis; these are the obstacles. Now listen to the mistaken notions of diet, O Parvati!

" 'That Samadhi (trance) can be at once induced by drinking certain new chemical essences and by eating certain kinds of food, is a mistake. Now hear about the mistaken notion of the influence of company.

" 'Keeping the company of the virtuous, and avoiding that of the vicious (is a mistaken notion). Measuring of the heaviness and lightness of the inspired and expired air (is an erroneous idea).

" 'Brahman is in the body or He is the maker of form, or He has a form, or He has no form, or He is everything—all these consoling doctrines are obstacles. Such notions are impediments in the shape of Jnana (Knowledge).'"

Yoga is defined as "the restraint of mental modifications".[11] For this the primary pre-requisite is posture, since without it peace of mind is impossible. Every bodily movement, twitch, or strain, every nerve impulse, as well as the flow of the breath, causes restlessness. Patanjali points out the necessity of posture, called 'asana' in Sanskrit, but he does not specify any particular form, for this is a matter to be settled according to the needs of each individual.[12] Any asana that is steady and pleasant is considered suitable. Vachaspati says 'asana' means "any position that may secure ease."[13]

In the famous tantrik treatise on Hatha Yoga, known as *Hatha Yoga Pradipika*, which I have used as the basis of this comparative treatment, opens its section on asanas as follows: "Being the first accessory of Hatha Yoga, asana is discussed first. It should be practised for gaining steady posture, health and lightness of body."[14] Without further comment the text describes the fifteen most important asanas adopted by such great Yogis as Vasistha and Matsyendra. This list is as follows: Svastiksana, Gomukhasana, Virasana, Kurmasana, Kukkutasana, Uttanakurmakasana, Dhanurasana, Matsyasana, Pascimottanasana, Mayurasana, Savasana, Siddhasana, Padmasana, Simhasana, and Bhadrasana.[15]

---

11) *The Yoga Sutras of Patanjali*, i, 2. Patanjali is considered to be the Father of Yoga, for it is believed that he first recorded systematically the practices.

12) The posture does not necessarily have to be a sitting one, for some are standing upright, lying down, bending or standing on the head. See also *Gheranda Samhita*, ii, 36, "Stand straight on one leg (the left), bending the right leg, and placing the right foot on the root of the left thigh; standing thus like a tree on the ground, is called the [Vrksasana] tree posture"; see Plate XXX. Ibid., 19: "Lying flat on the ground (on one's back) like a corpse is called the Mrtasana (Corpse-posture). This posture destroys fatigue, and quiets the agitation of the mind." This posture is sometimes called savasana. Compare *Hatha Yoga Pradipika*, i, 34: "Lying down on the ground like a corpse, is called Savasana. It removes fatigue and gives rest to the mind." In padhahasthasana the Yogi stands and touches his feet with his hands (see Plate XXXI). In vamadaksinapadasana the legs are brought up to right angles with the body, a kind of goose step. Other postures will be described further on.

13) *The Yoga Sutras of Patanjali*, ii, 46. Vachaspati is a famous commentator on *the Yoga Sutras of Patanjali*.

14) *Hatha Yoga Pradipika*, i, 19.

15) *Hatha Yoga Pradipika*, i. 21–57. The text points out that they are not all necessary. See 35–6: "Siva taught eighty-four asanas. Of these the first four being essential ones, I am going to explain them here. These four are Siddha, Padma, Simha, and Bhadra. Even of these, the Siddhasana being very comfortable, one should always practise it." Siddhasana and padmasana will be discussed more fully elsewhere. Simhasana is described in the text, i. 52–4: "Press the heels on both sides of the seam of the scrotum in such a way that the left heel touches the right side and the right heel touches the left side of it. Place the hands on the knees, with stretched fingers, and keeping the

The Gheranda Samhita, a tantrik work on Hatha Yoga, says:

There are eighty-four hundreds of thousands of Asanas described by Siva. The postures are as many in number as there are number of living creatures in this universe. Among them eighty-four are the best; and among these eighty-four, thirty-two have been found useful for mankind in this world. The thirty-two Asanas that give perfection in this mortal world are the following: Siddhasana (Perfect posture); Padmasana (Lotus posture); Bhadrasana (Gentle posture); Muktasana (Free posture); Vajrasana (Thunderbolt posture); Svastikasana (Prosperous posture); Simhasana (Lion posture); Gomukhasana (Cow-mouth posture); Virasana (Heroic posture); Dhanurasana (Bow posture); Mrtasana (Corpse posture); Guptasana (Hidden posture); Matsyasana (Fish posture); Matsyendrasana; Goraksasana; Pascimottanasana; Utkatasana (Hazardous posture); Samkatasana (Dangerous posture); Mayurasana (Peacock posture); Kukkutasana (Cock posture); Kurmasana (Tortoise posture); Uttana Kurmakasana; Uttana Mandukasana; Vrksasana (Tree posture); Mandukasana (Frog posture); Garudasana (Eagle posture); Vrsasana (Bull posture); Salabhasana (Locust posture); Makarasana (Dolphin posture); Ustrasana (Camel posture); Bhujangasana (Cobra posture); Yogasana.[16]

---

mouth open and the mind collected gaze on the tip of the nose. This is Simhasana, held secret by the best of Yogis. This excellent asana effects the completion of the three Bandhas. (Mulabandha, Kantha or Jalandhara Bandha and Uddiyana Bandha)."

Compare *Gheranda Samhita*, ii, 14–15: "The two heels to be placed under the scrotum contrariwise (i.e., left heel on the right side and the right heel on the left side of it) and turned upwards, the knees to be placed on the ground, and the hands placed on the knees, mouth to be kept open; practising the Jalandhara mudra one should fix his gaze on the tip of the nose. This is the Simhasana (Lion posture), the destroyer of all diseases."

For Bhadrasana see *Hatha Yoga Pradipika* i, 55–7: "Place the heels on either side of the seam of the scrotum, keeping the left heel on the left side and the right one on the right side, hold the feet firmly joined to one another with both the hands. This Bhadrasana is the destroyer of all the diseases. The expert Yogis call this Goraksasana. By sitting with this asana, the Yogi gets rid of fatigue."

Compare *Gheranda Samhita*, ii, 9–10: "Place the heels crosswise under the testes attentively; cross the hands behind the back and take hold of the toes of the feet. Fix the gaze on the tip of the nose, having previously adopted the Mudra called Jalandhara. This is the Bhadrasana (or happy posture) which destroys all sorts of disease." A different posture is described for Goraksasana in *Gheranda Samhita ii*, 24–5: "Between the knees and the thighs, the two feet turned upward and placed in a hidden way, the heels being carefully covered by the two hands outstretched; the throat being contracted, let one fix the gaze on the tip of the nose. This is called Goraksasana. It gives success to the Yogins."

16) Gheranda Samhita, ii, 1–6. Compare *Siva Samhita*, iii, 84: "There are eighty-four postures of various modes. Out of them, four ought to be adopted, which I mention below: — 1. Siddhasana; 2. Padmasana; 3. Ugrasana [Pascimottanasana]; 4. Svastikasana." All but the last of these postures will be given later. Svastikasana is described, iii, 95–7: "Place the soles of the feet completely under the thighs, keep the body straight and sit at ease. This is called the Svastikasana. In this way the wise Yogi should practise the regulation of the air. No disease can attack his body, and he obtains Vayu

In this literature many fantastic claims are made, and mystic panaceas are promised for each of the asanas and other disciplines of Yoga. Though many of them are believed in literally by contemporary Yogis, it is obvious that they are not the primary concern or aim of practical Yoga. Some of the classic claims are explained as familiar metaphors, others as possible benefits, but emphasis is put by the Yogi (at least, by my teacher) on the more tangible and direct benefits of body and mind. In what follows I have attempted to be as specific as possible in reproducing the interpretation of aims given by my own teacher, regardless of literary tradition.

There is not a single asana that is not intended directly or indirectly to quiet the mind; however, for the advanced meditation practices of Yoga there are only two postures that are considered essential. These are siddhasana and padmasana. The other asanas have been devised to build up different parts of the body and to develop the needed strength that is required by the rigid physical disciplines imposed upon the student. The postures are also used to keep the body in good health and to help the beginner overcome the monotony of his extremely sedentary life.

The teacher emphasizes that the primary purpose of the asanas is the reconditioning of the system, both mind and body, so as to effect the highest possible standard of muscular tone, mental health, and organic vigour. Hence stress is put upon the nervous and the glandular systems. Hatha Yoga is interpreted as a method that will achieve the maximum results by the minimum expenditure of energy. The various asanas have been devised primarily to stimulate, exercise, and massage the specific areas that demand attention. With these asanas, therefore, my account will begin.

Siddhi. This is also called the Sukhasana (the easy posture). This health-giving, good Svastikasana should be secret by the Yogi."

Compare *Gheranda Samhita*, ii, 13: "Drawing the legs and thighs together and placing the feet between them, keeping the body in its easy condition and sitting straight, constitute the posture called the Svastikasana."

Compare *Hatha Yoga Pradipika*, i , 21 "Having kept both the feet between the knees and the thighs, with body straight, when one sits calmly, it is called Svastikisana."

ASANAS

FIRST there was prescribed for me a group of asanas calculated to bring a rich supply of blood to the brain and to various parts of the spinal cord. They were sarvangasana (shoulder stand, see Plate I),[1] to supply the cervical region of the spine; halasana (plow posture, see Plate III),[2] the dorsal and lumbar regions; pascimottanasana (posterior stretching posture, see Plate VI),[3] the lumbar and sacral regions; mayurasana (peacock posture, see Plate VIII),[4] the upper lumbar and

---

1) Lie flat on the back and then lift the legs up in the air until the body is in a "shoulder stand." The trunk can be supported with the arms raised from the elbows. There is no mention of this posture in the traditional literature. For complete details see the volume on *Asanas*, by Srimat Kuvalayananda. pp. 73–5.

A complementary posture given to me to be practised with sarvangasana was matsyasana (fish posture, see Plate II). It is described in the Gheranda Samhita, ii, 21: "Make the Padmasana posture without the crossing of the arms; lie on the back, holding the head by the two elbows. This is the Matsyasana (Fish posture), the destroyer of diseases."

2) Lie in a supine position as in sarvangasana and then slowly lift the legs and extend the feet beyond the head. This bends and stretches the entire spinal cord and should be done cautiously. This posture is not given in the texts being compared. See Srimat Kuvalayananda, *Asanas*, pp. 78–81.

3) *See Hatha Yoga Pradipika*, i. 30–1: "Having stretched the legs on the ground, like sticks and having grasped the toes of both the feet with both the hands, when one sits with his forehead resting on the thighs, it is called Pascimottanasana. This foremost of Asanas, Pascimottanas, carries the air from the front to the back part of the body (i.e. to the susumna). It kindles gastric fire, reduces obesity and cures all diseases of men."

Compare *Gheranda Samhita*, ii, 26: "Stretch the two legs on the ground, stiff like a stick (the heels not touching), and place the forehead on the two knees, and catch with the hands the toes. This is called the Pascimottanasana."

Compare *Siva Samhita*, iii, 92–4: "Stretch out both the legs and keep them apart; firmly take hold of head by the hands and place them on the knees. This is called Ugrasana (the stern-posture), it excites the motion of the air, destroys the dullness and uneasiness of the body, and is also called Pascimottanasana (the posterior crossed posture). That wise man who daily practises this noble posture can certainly induce the flow of the air *per viam posteriori*. Those who practise this obtain all the Siddhis; therefore, those, desirous of attaining powers, should practise this diligently. This should be kept secret with the greatest care, and not be given to anybody and everybody. Through it, Vayu Siddhi is easily obtained, and it destroys a multitude of miseries!"

4) *Hatha Yoga Pradipika*, i, 32–3: "Place the palms of both the hands on the ground, and place the navel on both the elbows and balancing thus, the body should be stretched backward like a stick. This is called Mayurasana. This asana soon destroys all diseases and removes abdominal disorders, and also those arising from irregularities of phlegm, bile and wind, digests unwholesome

dorsal sections. I was also given a series of reconditioning asanas to stretch, bend, and twist the spinal cord in different ways, giving it a sort of massage which is intended to promote the health of the nerves rooted there. They were salabhasana (locust posture, see plate X),[5] bhujangasana (cobra posture, see plate XI),[6] and dhanurasana (bow posture, see plate XII).[7] The outstanding twisting posture was ardha matsyendrasana (half-spine twist, see plate XIII).[8]

---

food taken in excess, increases appetite and destroys the most deadly poison."

Compare *Gheranda Samhita*, ii, 29–30: "Place the palms of the two hands on the ground, place the umbilical region on the two elbows, stand upon the hands, the legs being raised in the air, and crossed like Padmasana. This is called the Mayurasana (Peacock posture [see Plate IX]). The Peacock posture destroys the effects of unwholesome food; it produces heat in the stomach; it destroys the effects of deadly poisons; it easily cures diseases like Gulma (enlargement of the spleen) and fever; such is this useful posture." I found this posture particularly useful when flushing the colon after doing basti (a mudra to be described later). When I used it for this purpose the legs were spread apart in order to relax the anal sphincters.

5) *Gheranda Samhita*, ii, 39: "Lie on the ground face downwards, the two hands being placed on the chest, touching the ground with the palms, raise the legs in the air one cubit high. This is called the Salabhasana (Locust posture)." A variation of this posture is described in ibid., ii, 40; "Lie on the ground face downwards, the chest touching the earth, the two legs being stretched; catch the head with the two arms. This is Makarasana, the increaser of the bodily heat."

6) *Ibid.*, 42–3: "Let the body, from the navel downwards to the toes, touch the ground, place the palms on the ground, raise the head (the upper portion of the body) like a serpent. This is called Bhujangasana (Cobra posture). This always increases the bodily heat, destroys all diseases, and by the practice of this posture the serpent-goddess (the kundalini force) awakes!"

7) *Hatha Yoga Pradipika*, i, 27: "Having caught the big toes of the feet with both the hands and carried them to the ears by drawing up the body like a bow, it becomes Dhanurasana." Compare *Gheranda Samhita*, ii, 18: "…stretching the legs on the ground like a stick, and catching hold of (the toes of) the feet with the hands, and making the body like a bow, is called the Dhanurasana (Bow posture)." The posture taught to me as the 'bow posture' is described here as ustraasana. See 41: "Lie on the ground face downwards, turn up the legs and place them towards the back, catch the legs with the hands, contract forcibly the mouth and the abdomen. This is called the Ustrasana (Camel posture)."

8) *Hatha Yoga Pradipika*, i, 28–9: "Having placed the right foot at the root of the left thigh, let the toe be grasped with the right hand passing over the back, and having placed the left foot on the right thigh at its root, let it be grasped with the left hand passing behind the back. This is the asana, as explained by Sri Matsyanatha. It increases appetite, and is an instrument for destroying the group of the most deadly diseases. Its practice awakens the Kundalini, and stops the nectar shedding from the moon in people." I was given this posture as the complete lotus posture (baddha padmasana). Compare *Gheranda Samhita*, ii. 22–3: "Keeping the abdominal region at ease like the back, bending the left leg, place it on the right thigh, then place on this the elbow of the right hand, and place the face on the palm of the right hand and fix the gaze between the eye-brows. This is called the Matsyendra posture." The posture taught to me under this name was different from those described in the texts. Place the left foot at the root of the right thigh, then put the right foot on the other side of the left thigh, and catch hold of the left knee with the left hand. Next rotate the body

At first it was almost impossible to execute these positions; however, by the end of the first month, I was able to assume them without any effort. Several months passed before I was able to hold them with ease. I was permitted to vary the order in any way I found suitable. For the most part, I began with pascimottanasana, because it warmed up the system quicker than any other asanas; however, I did not attempt the full posture until the perspiration began to flow. For the first few minutes I was satisfied to place my hands on my ankles and let my head comes as close to the knees as was comfortable without forcing it. I tried to hold each posture ten seconds and then repeated the practice five times. This was enough in the beginning. Later I increased the time until I could hold each position comfortably for one minute, repeating them ten times without fatigue. After I developed sufficient strength to hold sarvangasana, I raised the time to fifteen minutes instead of repeating it several times, as l did with all the other asanas.

Having performed the reconditioning asanas, I undertook the meditation asanas themselves, in order to acquire the necessary flexibility to do them with ease. The most outstanding of these, which I used exclusively, are siddhasana and padmasana. Every student is required to learn them. Siddhasana (see Plate XV) is described in the text.[9] It

to the right and arrange the upper portion of the left arm so that it is on the right side of the right knee, which is used as a fulcrum to help twist the body. Place the right arm around the back as far as possible, looking out over the right shoulder. The reverse of this is also practised.

9)   See *Hatha Yoga Pradipika*, i. 37–45: "Press firmly the heel of the left foot against the perineum, and the right heel above the male organ. With the chin pressing on the chest one should sit tight, having restrained the senses, and gaze steadily at the space between the eyebrows. This is called Siddhasana, the Opener of the Door of Salvation. This Siddhasana is performed also by placing the left heel on the Medhra (above the male organ) and then placing the right one on it. Some call this Siddhasana; some Vajrasana. Others call it Muktasana or Guptasana. Just as sparing food is among Yamas, and Ahimsa among the Niyamas, so is Siddhasana called by adepts the chief of all asanas. Out of the 84 asanas Siddhasana should always be practised, because it cleanses the impurities of 72,000 nadis [nerves]. By contemplating on oneself, by eating sparingly, and by practising Siddhasana for 12 years, the Yogi obtains success. Other postures are of no use, when success is achieved in Siddhasana, and Prana Vayu [breath] becomes calm and restrained by Kevala Kumbhaka [a form of breath suspension to be discussed later]. Success in Siddhasana alone becoming firmly established one gets Unmani [mindlessness] at once, and the other three seats (Bandhas) are accomplished of themselves. There is no asana like the Siddhasana and no Kumbhaka like the Kevala. There is no Mudra like the Khecari and no Laya like the Nada (Anahata Nada — Heart Sound)"

Compare *Gheranda Samhita*, ii, 7: "The practitioner who has subdued his passions, having placed one heel at the anal aperture should keep the other heel on the root of the generative organ; afterwards he should rest his chin upon the chest, and being quiet and straight, gaze at the spot between the two eyebrows. This is called the Siddhasana which leads to emancipation."

was not very difficult; being a simple cross-legged posture, I mastered it quickly. The three asanas mentioned below in the quotation from *Hatha Yoga Pradipika*, namely, vajrasana, muktasana, and guptasana, were taught to me as separate postures.[10] The names suggest what the posture looks like or emphasizes. I learned these three as separate postures and found them highly efficacious. According to the instructions given to me the only difference among the meditation postures is the point in the body at which pressure is exerted in order to stimulate or check the flow of nervous energy. With these I also used simhasana, bhadrasana, goraksasana, and svastikasana which have been described in previous references; other associated postures which were required in my schedule are given below.[11]

Compare *Siva Samhita*, iii, 85–7: "The Siddhasana that gives success to the practitioner is as follows:—Pressing with care by the heel the Yoni, the Yogi should place the other heel on the Lingam; he should fix his gaze upwards on the space between the eyebrows, should be steady, and restrain his senses. His body particularly must be straight and without any bend. The place should be a retired one, without any noise. He who wishes to attain quick consummation of Yoga, by exercise, should adopt the Siddhasana posture, and practise regulation of the breath. Through this posture the Yogi, leaving the world, attains the highest end and throughout the world there is no posture more secret than this. By assuming and contemplating in this posture, the Yogi is freed from sin."

10) In *Gheranda Samhita* they are described separately. See ii, 12: "Make the thighs tight like vajra and place the legs by the two sides of the anus. This is called the Vajrasana (thunderbolt posture — see Plate XVI). It gives psychic powers to the Yogin." This posture may also be done in the supine position (see Plate XVII). A further development of this posture is to incline the trunk backward until the head rests on the floor (see Plate XVIII), then return the body to an erect sitting position. In the beginning I used my arms to let the trunk down slowly, finally resting on my elbows. After ten seconds in this position, I returned my body to its former position with the aid of my arms. I repeated this exercise ten times, and after a few weeks I was able to execute it without the use of the arms.

Ibid., 11 : "Place the left heel at the root of the organ of generation and the right heel above that, keep the head and the neck straight with the body. This posture is called the Muktasana (free posture). It gives Siddhi (perfection)."

Ibid., 20: "Hide the two feet between the knees and thighs, and place the anus on the feet. This is known as the Guptasana (hidden posture)." Some teachers call it samasana, or the symmetrical pose.

11) "See *Gheranda Samhita*, ii, 27: "Let the toes touch the ground and the heels be raised in the air; place the anus on the heels; this is known as the Utkatasana [hazardous posture]."

Ibid., 28: "Placing the left foot and the leg on the ground, surround the left foot by the right leg; and place the two hands on the two knees. This is the Samkatasana [dangerous posture; see Plate XIX]."

Ibid., "Place the heels contrariwise under the scrotum, stiffen (or keep at ease) the head, neck and body. This is called the [Kurmasana] Tortoise posture." Compare *Hatha Yoga Pradipika*, i. 24. "Placing the right ankle on the left side of the anus, and the left ankle on the right side of it, making what the Yogis call Kurmasana."

Ibid., 34: "Carry the feet towards the back, the toes touching each other, and place the knees forwards. This is called the [Mandukasana] Frog posture."

The most universally used, as well as one of the most difficult of the asanas is padmasana (see frontispiece), which is fully discussed in the text.[12] Many months were required for the perfection of this

---

Ibid., 35: "Assume the Frog posture, holding the head by the elbows, and stand up like a frog. This is called the Uttanamandukasana."

Ibid., 37: "Place the legs and the thighs on the ground press it, steady the body with the two knees, place the two hands on the knees; this is called the Garudasana [Garuda is a mythical bird]."

Ibid., 38: "Place the anus on the right heel, on the left of it place the left leg crossing it opposite way, and touch the ground. This is called the [Vrsasana] Bull posture."

Ibid., 16: "The two feet to be placed on the ground, and the heels to be placed contrariwise under the buttocks; the body to be kept steady and the mouth raised, and sitting equably; this is called the Gomukhasana: resembling the mouth of a cow." Compare *Hatha Yoga Pradipika*, i, 22: "Placing the right ankle on the left side of the back and the left ankle on the right side, makes Gomukhasana, causing the appearance of the mouth of a cow."

12) See *Hatha Yoga Pradipika*, i. 46–51: "Place the right foot on the left thigh and the left foot on the right thigh, and grasp the big toes firmly with the hands crossed over the back. Press the chin against the chest, and gaze on the tip of the nose. This is called Padmasana, the destroyer of the diseases of the Yamis (practisers). [This was given to me as the perfected lotus posture, called baddha Padmasana —see Plate XX.]

"Place the feet on the thighs, with the soles upwards, and place the hands on the thighs, with the palms upward, gaze on the tip of the nose, keeping the tongue pressed against the root of the two upper central teeth, and the chin against the chest, and raise the air up, i.e. pull the apana-vayu gently upwards. This is called the Padmasana, the destroyer of all diseases. It is difficult of attainment, but can be learned by intelligent people in this world. Having kept both the hands together in the lap, performing the Padmasana firmly, keeping the chin fixed to the chest and contemplating on Him in the mind, be drawing the apana-vayu (performing Mula Bandha) and pushing down the air after inhaling it, joining thus the prana and apana in the navel, one gets the highest intelligence by awakening the Sakti (kundalini) thus. The Yogi who, sitting in Padmasana, can control breathing, there is no doubt, is free from bondage."

Compare *Gheranda Samhita*, ii, 8: "Place the right foot on the left thigh and similarly the left one on the right thigh, also cross the hands behind the back and firmly catch hold of the great toes of the feet so crossed. Place the chin on the chest and fix the gaze on the tip of the nose. This posture is called the Padmasana (Lotus posture). This posture destroys all diseases."

Compare *Siva Samhita*, iii, 88–91: "I describe now the Padmasana which wards off (or cures) all diseases:—Having crossed the legs, carefully place the feet on the opposite thighs (i.e., the left foot on the right thigh, and vice versa); cross both the hands and place them similarly on the thighs and sight on the tip of the nose; pressing the tongue against the root of the teeth (the chin should be elevated, the chest expanded); then draw the air slowly, fill the chest with all your might, and expel slowly, in an unobstructed stream. It cannot be practised by everybody; only the wise attain success in it. By performing and practising this posture, undoubtedly the vital airs of the practitioner at once become completely equable and flow harmoniously through the body. Sitting in the Padmasana posture, and knowing the action of the Prana and Apana, when the Yogi performs the regulation of the breath, he is emancipated. I tell you the truth. Verily, I tell you the truth."

An associated posture is virasana (hero posture; see Plate XXII), *Hatha Yoga Pradipika*, i, 23: "One foot is to be placed on the thigh of the opposite side; and so also the other foot under the opposite thigh. This is called Virasana."

Compare *Gheranda Samhita*, ii, 17: "One leg (the right foot) to be placed on the other (left thigh), and the other foot to be turned backwards. This is called Virasana (Hero posture)."

posture. By 'perfection' I mean the state of accomplishment given by Vyasa, "posture becomes perfect when effort to that end ceases, so that there may be no more movement of the body."[13] The requirement that the posture must be held for three hours is the chief difficulty and makes intelligible why it took so long to achieve it. At first it seemed impossible, but it was not long before the results of my efforts began to appear. I started by holding the posture one minute and added a minute each week. At the end of the first month I felt comfortable in the posture for five minutes. By the end of the second month I was able to maintain it for fifteen minutes. From this point on I made it a practice to assume padmasana whenever there was an opportunity. This enabled me to repeat it several times a day. The real stumbling block was reached when I was able to hold the position half an hour, for it seemed impossible to go beyond this point without suffering. In order to increase the time I made it a habit to sit in the cross-legged position whenever I was studying. Only in this way was I eventually able to raise the time limit. It is not absolutely necessary to develop padmasana to this degree; however, there is no doubt about its importance in the advanced breathing practices. For all practical meditation purposes, I found siddhasana to be sufficient; so there is no need to be over anxious if padmasana seems impossible.

When I was able to execute padmasana, I was instructed to practise the following series of allied postures: kukkutasana (see Plate XXIII), uttanakurmakasana (see Plate XXIV), yogasana (see Plate XXV), vajroli mudra (see Plate XXVI), and pasini mudra (see Plate XXVII).[14]

---

13) *The Yoga Sutras of Patanjali*, ii. 47: Vyasa is one of the outstanding commentators on *the Yoga Sutras of Patanjali*.

14) *Hatha Yoga Pradipika*, i, 25: "Taking the posture of Padmasana and carrying the hands between the knees and the thighs, when the Yogi raises himself above the ground, with his palms resting on the ground, it becomes Kukkutasana."
Compare *Gheranda Samhita*, ii. 31: "Sitting on the ground, cross the legs in the Padmasana posture, thrust down the hands between the thighs and the knees, stand on the hands, supporting the body on the elbows. This is called the Kukkutasana (Cock posture)."
Hatha Yoga Pradipika, i, 26: "Having assumed Kukkutasana, when one grasps his neck by crossing his hands behind his back, and lies in this posture like a tortoise, with his back touching the ground, it becomes Uttanakurmasana."
Compare *Gheranda Samhita*, ii, 33: "Assume the Cock Posture, catch hold of the neck with the hands, and stand stretched like a tortoise. This is the Uttanakurmakasana."
Ibid., 44–5: "Turn the feet upwards, place them on the knees; then place the hands on the ground with the palms turned upwards; inspire, and fix the gaze on the tip of the nose. This is called the Yoga Posture assumed by the Yogins when practising Yoga"

I was told to develop the last two at this time so that I should have sufficient strength to use them in the more advanced stages. The photographs explain them sufficiently.

One of the most important postures that I was required to perfect is called sirsasana (head stand, see Plate XXVIII) and deserves special comment. This posture is not listed in the texts as an asana, but it is described among the mudras under the name viparita karani (inverted body).[15] Regardless of the name used, it is one of the preliminaries that students are required to learn. Since it was assigned to me when I was learning the asanas, I choose to speak of it here. As in the attainment of all asanas, I was advised to proceed with due caution. My teacher assured me that there is no danger for anyone in a normal state of health who is mindful of every change that takes place and allows ample time for the system to accommodate itself to the inverted position. At first it seemed hopeless, especially when I found that the standard for perfection is three hours. To accomplish this goal without any setbacks, my teacher advised me to start with ten seconds for the first week and then to add thirty seconds each week until I brought the time up to fifteen minutes. This required several months. At this point I was advised to repeat the practice twice a day, which gave me a total of thirty minutes. After one month I added a midday practice

---

Ibid., iii, 45: "Place the two palms on the ground, raise the legs in the air upward, the head not touching the earth. This awakens the Sakti, causes long life, and is called Vajroli by the sages."

Ibid., iii. 84: "Throw the two legs on the neck towards the back, holding them strongly together like a Pasa (a noose). This is called Pasini Mudra; it awakens the Sakti (kundalini)."

15) See *Hatha Yoga Pradipika,* iii. 78–81: "Above the navel and below the palate respectively, are the Surya and the Chandra. The exercise, called the Viparita Karani [inverted body], is learnt from the guru's instructions. This exercise increases the appetite; and, therefore, one who practises it, should obtain a good supply of food. If the food be scanty, the fire will burn him at once. Place the head on the ground and the feet up into the sky, for a second only the first day, and increase this time daily. After six months wrinkles and grey hair are not seen. He who practises it daily, even for three hours, conquers death." To obtain these benefits one must be an accomplished Yogi.

Compare *Gheranda Samhita,* iii, 33–5: "The sun (the solar Nadi or plexus) dwells at the root of the navel, and the moon at the root of the palate; as the sun eats up the nectar man becomes subject to death. The process by which the sun is brought upwards and the moon carried downward is called Viparitakarani. It is a sacred Mudra in all the Tantras. Place the head on the ground, with hands spread, raise the legs up, and thus remain steady. This is called Viparitakarani."

Compare *Siva Samhita,* iv, 45–7: "Putting the head on the ground, let him stretch out his legs upwards, moving them round and round. This is Viparita Karani, kept secret in all the Tantras. The Yogi who practices it daily for three hours, conquers death, and is not destroyed even in the Pralaya [Dissolution of the Universe at the end of a world period]. He who drinks nectar becomes equal to Siddhas; he who practises this Bandha becomes an adept among all creatures."

period and increased the duration to twenty minutes, which gave me one hour for the day. Thereafter I added five minutes each week until I brought up the time to a single practice period, which amounted to three hours for the day. In order further to increase the time for each period, I was advised to stop the midday practice and increase the duration of the other two periods. Eventually I abandoned the evening turn and held the posture for three hours at one time.

Immediately after standing on my head my breath rate speeded up; then it slowly subsided, and a general feeling of relaxation was experienced. Next came a tendency to restlessness. I had a desire to move my legs in different directions. Soon after this my body became warm and the perspiration began to flow. I was told that this was the measure of my capacity and that I should never try to hold the posture beyond this point. As my body grew stronger, a longer period of time was required for the manifestation of this nervousness. When this tendency was overcome, I was permitted to increase the duration.

One of the most trying problems I encountered when building up to the higher time standards was what to do with my mind. The moment I began to feel the slightest fatigue, my mind began to wander. At this point my teacher instructed me to select a spot on a level with my eyes, when standing on my head and direct the attention of my mind to it. Shortly this became a habit, and my mind adapted itself without the least awareness of the passage of time—in fact, I was eventually able to remain on my head for an hour and longer with no more knowledge of time than when I was asleep.

I was given a series of practices to be used when standing on my head. Interlock the feet, as in padmasana, then slowly lower the limbs until the knees touch the arms (see Plate XXIX), and then return the interlocked legs to the original perpendicular position without losing balance.[16] I performed this ten times and can highly recommend it for developing the abdominal muscles. In order to maintain one's balance during this exercise, each movement must be done with care and caution. I went through the same motions without interlocking the legs. While standing on my head, with feet together, I bent my legs forward until my toes touched the floor in front of me and then returned them to the perpendicular position. I was also allowed to stretch my legs

---

16)   This variation is not mentioned in the traditional literature. For further details see *Asanas* pp. 69–72.

while on my head. Separate them by doing 'a split', and then revolve the trunk until the legs completely reverse their first position. These practices are to relieve the monotony and at the same time to develop other muscles of the body. The entire routine requires only a few minutes, and I found it an excellent help in the early stages to build up my strength. The greatest need in all posture work is a capacity for endurance, and such measures are highly advisable.

All that is needed in the way of apparatus is a small mat or rug. Anything that is solid will serve the purpose, for the seat must be firm and the spine erect. It is not advisable to practise after eating; so a period in the day should be selected when the stomach is empty. Mid-afternoon meets this requirement. The body should be warm, so that there is no danger of straining the muscles. It is even recommended that one practise in warm water; however, in the United States it will be sufficient to practise after a sun bath, when the perspiration has begun to flow. According to Yogic theory, if all excess moisture is eliminated from the body and the joints, the postures can be taken more easily and the body will be subject to less pain.

For all asanas it is enough merely to assume the posture in the beginning. Repeat this three to five times and then take another asana. After a week or so, it will be possible to hold each asana for ten or fifteen seconds. From this point on take measured steps and always stay far within the bounds of caution.

No special order seems to be required. I was permitted to vary the asanas according to my own desire. In general I followed the sequence in which they have been here related, doing the head stand last. When working on the asanas I was in the habit of devoting from an hour to an hour and one-half to this. As I became more proficient and strove to maintain a particular posture for an extended period, as in the case of the head stand, the time had to be lengthened. For the sake of variety and to ensure the development of all the muscles, I included in my schedule from time to time some of the associated asanas. Eventually I became familiar with all of them, but at no time did I do them all in one session.

Since my training has not been done under laboratory conditions, I can only report general observations. The most noticeable effect was an excellent physical tone. The muscles became solid, all fat disappeared, and I enjoyed a feeling of well-being, with the mental results of such a condition. Undoubtedly scientific investigation could reveal many physiological factors that would help to explain the effects which in this work I must be content merely to describe.

P U R I F I C A T I O N

THE PURPOSE of Hatha Yoga is to gain control of the breath, but this is not possible until the body is thoroughly purified. The text opens its section on pranayama with the following quotation:

Posture becoming established, a Yogi, master of himself, eating salutary and moderate food,[1] should practise pranayama, as instructed by his guru.[2] …when the whole system of nadis which is full of impurities, is cleaned, then the Yogi becomes able to conserve the Prana.[3]… By removing the impurities of the nadis, the air can be restrained, according to one's wish, and the appetite is increased, the divine sound is awakened, and the body becomes healthy. If there be excess of fat or phlegm in the body, the six kinds of kriyas (duties) should be performed first. But others, not suffering from the excess of these, should not perform them. The six kinds are: Dhauti, Neti, Trataka,[4] Nauli, and Kapala Bhati. These are called the six actions.[5]

---

1) *Hatha Yoga Pradipika*, i, 60: "Abstemious feeding is that in which three fourths of hunger is satisfied with food, well cooked with ghee (clarified butter), and sweets, and eaten with the offering of it to Siva." Compare Gheranda Samhita, v, 21-2: "…pure, sweet and cooling food should be eaten to fill half the stomach; eating thus sweet juices with pleasure and leaving the other half of the stomach empty is called moderation in diet. Half the stomach should be filled with food, one quarter with water; and one quarter should be kept empty for practising pranayama."

2) *Hatha Yoga Pradipika*; ii, I.

3) Compare *Gheranda Samhita*, v, 34–5: The student asked the teacher, "Ocean of mercy! How are nadis purified, what is the purification of nadis; I want to learn all this; recite to me." Gheranda, the teacher, said, "The vayu does not (cannot) enter the nadis so long as they are full of impurities. How then can Pranayama be accomplished? How can there be knowledge of Tattvas (subtle forces of nature)? Therefore, first the Nadis should be purified, and then Pranayama should be practised."

4) This practice was not included in my discipline for the purification of the body, but I had to learn it during my preliminary training period as a preparation for the advanced meditation exercises. The technique is simple. *Hatha Yoga Pradipika*, ii, 31-2: "Being calm, one should gaze steadily at a small mark, till the eyes are filled with tears. This is called Trataka by acharyas. Trataka destroys the eye diseases and removes sloth, etc. It should be kept secret very carefully, like a box of jewellery." Compare *Gheranda Samhita*, i, 53–4: "Gaze steadily without winking at any small object, until the tears begin to flow. This is called Trataka or Gazing by the wise. By practising this Yoga, Sambhavi Mudra is obtained; and certainly all diseases of the eye are destroyed and clairvoyance is induced."

5) *Hatha Yoga Pradipika*, ii, 1–22, Compare *Gheranda Samhita*, i, 12. This text lists the six purification processes: "Dhauti, Vasti, Neti, Lauliki, Trataka, Kapalabhati are the Satkarmas or six practices,

I was required to learn these six kriyas before entering the retreat. It is customary to devote from one to three months to this preparatory period; in my case it took about three weeks, since I had been engaged in physical training previously. Everyone must learn these simple techniques. By taking up one at a time and giving it a little attention every day, I found no difficulty in mastering them.

'Dhauti' means to wash, clean, or purify. The Yogi is particularly concerned with the inside of his body; a simple technique of purification has been devised. "A strip of cloth, about three inches wide and fifteen cubits long, moistened with warm water, should be slowly swallowed in the way shown by the guru, and should be taken out again. This is called Dhauti Karma."[6] The importance assigned in tradition

---

known as Sadhana." Inconsistencies will be discussed later. The importance of these practices is indicated by the position they command in this authoritative text.

6) *Hatha Yoga Pradipika*, ii, 24. Compare *Gheranda Samhita*, i, 13–44: "The Dhautis are of four kinds, and they clear away the impurities of the body. They are (A) Antardhauti (internal washing); (B) Dantadhauti (cleaning the teeth); (C) Hrd-dhauti (cleaning the chest); (D) Mulasodhana (cleaning the rectum). (A) ANTAR-DHAUTI is again subdivided into four parts: Vatasara (wind purification), Varisara (water purification), Vahnisara (fire purification), and Bahiskrta. VATASARA-DHAUTI: contract the mouth like the beak of a crow and drink air slowly, and filling the stomach slowly with it, move it therein, and then slowly force it out through the lower passage. The Vatasara is a very secret process, it causes the purification of the body, it destroys all diseases and increases the gastric fire. VARISARA-DHAUTI: fill the mouth with water down to the throat, and then drink it slowly; and then move it through the stomach, forcing it downwards expelling it through the rectum. This process should be kept very secret. It purifies the body. And by practising it with care, one gets a luminous or shining body. The Varisara is the highest Dhauti. He who practises it with ease, purifies his filthy body and turns it into a shining one. AGNISARA or Fire Purification: press in the navel knot or intestines towards the spine for one hundred times. This is Agnisara or fire process. This gives success in the practice of Yoga, it cures all the diseases of the stomach (gastric juice) and increases the internal fire. This form of Dhauti should be kept very secret, and it is hardly to be attained even by the gods. By this Dhauti alone one certainly gets a luminous body. BAHISKRTA-DHAUTI: by Kakacancu or crow-bill Mudra fill the stomach with air, hold it there for one hour and a half, and then force it down towards the intestines. This Dhauti must be kept a great secret, and must not be revealed to anybody. Then standing in navel-deep water, draw out the Saktinadi (long intestines), wash the Nadi with hands so long as its filth is not all washed away; wash it with care, and then draw it in again into the abdomen. This process should be kept secret. It is not easily to be attained even by the gods. Simply by this Dhauti one gets Deva-deha (Godlike body). As long as a person has not the power of retaining the breath for an hour and a half (or retaining wind in the stomach for that period) so long he cannot achieve this grand Dhauti or purification, known as Bahiskrtadhauti. (B) DANTA-DHAUTI, or Teeth Purification. Danta-Dhauti is of five kinds; washing of the teeth, of the tongue, of the root of the tongue, of the mouth of each of the two eustachian tubes and of the frontal sinuses. DANTA-MULA-DHAUTI: rub the teeth with catechu-powder or with pure earth, so long as dental impurities are not removed. This teeth-washing is a great Dhauti and an important process in the practice of Yoga for the Yogins. It should be done daily in the morning by the Yogins, in order to preserve the teeth. In purification this is approved of by the Yogins. JIHVA-SODHANA, or Tongue Dhauti: I shall now tell the method of cleans-

to this practice is seen from the next verse, "there is no doubt that cough, asthma, enlargement of the spleen, leprosy and, twenty kinds of diseases born of phlegm disappear by the practice of Dhauti Karma."[7]

Begin with a small piece of cloth about three feet long. I found that an ordinary four-inch surgeon's gauze met every requirement. First put the cloth in a basin of water, and after it is thoroughly saturated insert one end of it as far back in the throat as possible and go through the motions of eating and swallowing. This will encourage the throat to take hold. There may be some spasms, but they will soon pass, as will all soreness that is experienced. It will take only a few days for the throat and stomach to accommodate themselves. Do not try to accomplish the feat on the first day. I began with a few inches and increased the length a little each day until I had swallowed the required twenty-

---

ing the tongue. The elongation of the tongue destroys old age, death and disuse. Join together the three fingers known as the index, the middle and the ring finger, put them into the throat, and rub well and clean the root of the tongue, and by washing it again throw out the phlegm. Having thus washed it rub it with butter, and milk it again and again; then by holding the tip of the tongue with an iron instrument pull it out slowly and slowly. Do this daily with diligence before the rising and setting sun. By so doing, the tongue becomes elongated. KARNA-DHAUTI, or Ear-Cleaning: Clean the two holes of the ears by the index and the ring fingers. By practising it daily, the mystical sounds are heard. KAPALA- RANDHRA-DHAUTI: Rub with the thumb of the right hand the depression in the forehead near the bridge of the nose. By the practice of this Yoga, diseases arising from derangements of phlegmatic humours are cured. The vessels become purified and clairvoyance is induced. This should be practised daily after awakening from sleep, after meals, and in the evening. (C) HRD-DHAUTI: Hrd-dhauti, or purification of the chest (or rather the throat) is of three kinds, viz., by a Danda (a stick), Vamana (vomiting), and by Vasas (cloth). DANDA-DHAUTI: Take either a plantain stalk or a stalk of turmeric (Haridra) or a stalk of cane, and thrust it slowly into the gullet and then draw it out slowly. By this process all the phlegm, bile and other impurities arc expelled out of the mouth. By this Danda-Dhauti every kind of heart-disease is surely cured. VAMANA-DHAUTI: After meal, let the wise practitioner drink water full up to the throat, then looking for a short while upwards, let him vomit it out again. By daily practising this Yoga, disorders of the phlegm and bile are cured. VASO-DHAUTI: let him swallow slowly a thin cloth, four fingers wide, then let him draw it out again. This is called Vaso-Dhauti. This cures Gulma or abdominal diseases, fever, enlarged spleen, leprosy, and other diseases and disorders of phlegm and bile, and day by day the practitioner gets health, strength, and cheerfulness. (D) MULA-SODHANA or Purification of the Rectum: The Apanavayu does not flow freely so long as the rectum is not purified. Therefore, with the greatest care let him practise this purification of the large intestines. By the stalk of the root of Haridra (turmeric) or the middle finger, the rectum should be carefully cleansed with water over and over again. This destroys constipation, indigestion, and dyspepsia, and increases the beauty and vigour of the body and enkindles the sphere of the fire (i.e., the gastric juice)." It is quite unnecessary for the student to practise every one of these techniques. Those that are of outstanding importance will be treated separately.

7) *Hatha Yoga Pradipika*, ii. 25. To understand such statements, one should study the Indian form of medicine called aryuveda. The most authoritative texts are Susruta, which is in three volumes, and Charaka, which is in four volumes. To be independent of a teacher, a student must make an exhaustive study of this subject.

two and one-half feet. With a little patience, anyone can master the technique in about three weeks.

I practised ten to fifteen minutes each day, after which, regardless of success, I discontinued the discipline until the following day. In this way there was no undue strain imposed upon the delicate lining of the throat. The first task is to accommodate the muscles to this foreign intrusion. When this has been done, time and practice will develop the needed strength to swallow the entire cloth. To overcome the difficulty encountered at the initial stage, I found it helpful to sweeten the water in which the cloth was moistened. On a few occasions I soaked it in milk.

Extracting the cloth is the simplest part of the procedure. The problem is to make it remain in the stomach, for as soon as it accumulates, there is a tendency to throw it out. I found that after I had rested for a few seconds the spasms passed away. Once the cloth has been swallowed, the stomach should be churned in order to ensure a thorough cleansing. Then bend over a basin and gently pull the loose end of the strip of cloth, while holding the mouth in a gasping position. If the throat contracts, pause for a few seconds and it will relax its grip. Do not pull hard, for there is nothing to fear. After a few days it was possible for me to execute the entire procedure without the slightest difficulty.

Experience makes it advisable to caution that if one uses the regular four-inch surgeon's gauze it is a safety-first measure to tie a knot at the point of the measured length to be used and then to leave three or four feet extra to remain unswallowed. In perfecting these practices the student becomes more bold, and frequently curiosity causes many unexpected problems. One might try to swallow up to the last quarter of an inch and by some rare accident he might let the end slip and find himself with a stomach full of cloth and no end to pull. If this should happen, the problem would be, not the stomach, but the mind, for the student will envision all sorts of fantastic doom. This has happened to me, hence these words of caution. In such an event, drink a strong solution of salt water or any other emetic, and the stomach will expel it immediately. After the cloth has been in the stomach twenty minutes or so, it will start to move out, passing through the pyloric valve. Even so, there is nothing to fear. Pull lightly and the muscles will release their grip. To evade all such unnecessary catastrophes, do not leave the cloth in the stomach more than twenty minutes and always leave a couple of feet of the cloth unswallowed.

By following these directions the average student will be able to learn this technique in three weeks. However, I found that I needed a full month in order to acquire sufficient strength to swallow the entire cloth in ten minutes, which is the usual time allotted to this performance. One should practise this technique another month or two; afterward he can set it aside and try to master another. If a long period of time passes before there is occasion to practise it again, it will take only a few days to accustom the throat to the cloth. No special difficulties will arise.

It is customary to practise this every morning during the preparatory period of the retreat. After the system has been thoroughly cleansed and the new pattern of living has been established, it can be dispensed with. However, I was advised to continue it until I had become proficient in the practice of pranayama.

There is another form of dhauti that one can learn to advantage, especially when no cloth is available. It is called vamana dhauti.[8] The technique is simple. Drink eight or nine glassfuls of water, or enough so that it backs up into the throat. This will create a feeling of nausea, making it easy to empty the stomach of its entire contents. In the beginning, in order completely to evacuate the stomach, I had to massage the root of the tongue with the fingers. After a little practice it was possible to empty the stomach voluntarily. When this stage had been reached, I had only to drink a few glasses of water and churn the stomach for a few minutes in order to wash the stomach.

The next important technique described in the text for cleansing the body is basti.

Squatting in navel-deep water, and introducing a six-inch-long smooth piece of half an inch diameter pipe, open at both ends, half inside the anus; it (anus) should be contracted and the water drawn up and then expelled. This washing is called the Basti Karma (Syringe-action). By practising this Basti Karma, colic, enlarged

---

8) *Gheranda Samhita*, i. 39. See previous reference for classical description. For the dry forms see *ibid.,* iii. 86–7: "Contract the lips, like the beak of a crow, and drink (draw in) the air slowly and slowly. This is Kaki (crow) mudra, destroyer of all diseases. The Kaki-mudra is a great Mudra, kept secret in all Tantras. By virtue of this, one becomes free from disease like a crow." *Ibid.,* 92–3: "Extending the face a little forward, let him drink (draw in) air through the gullet; this is called Bhujangini Mudra (Serpent-Mudra), destroyers of decay and death. This Serpent-mudra quickly destroys all stomach diseases, especially indigestion, dyspepsia, etc."

spleen and dropsy, arising from the disorders of vata (air), pitta (bile) and kapha (phlegm)[9] are all cured. By practising Basti with water the Dhatus,[10] the Indriyas[11] and the mind become clear. It gives glow and tone to the body and increases the appetite. All the disorders disappear.[12]

When one undertakes to learn basti, it is assumed that nauli and asvini mudra have already been mastered. These are explained later.[13] The student will then encounter no problem in accomplishing the technique described in the text. It can be performed by using an ordinary nozzle from an enema bag and a bathtub full of water. Insert the nozzle while squatting in the tub in water navel high, and then do nauli. I found that I was able to get the desired results on the first attempt. The isolation of the recti muscles by nauli creates a vacuum which sucks in the water. When the breath is gone, withdraw the nozzle and rest a moment; then repeat the practice. It takes only a few seconds to draw in sufficient water; so one should be able to do it within one breath. This is only a matter of convenience, so breathe as many times as is comfortable.

I was required to learn how to execute this technique without the aid of the nozzle, as follows: Place the feet about one foot apart and assume a squatting position with the arms locked around the flexed

---

9) These are the basic principles of their system of physiology. See *Susruta*, Introduction and *passim*.

10) These are the fundamental constituents of the body: chyle, blood, flesh, fat, bone, marrow, and semen. See *Susruta*, Introduction and *passim*.

11) 'Indriyas' means the faculties of perception and action. They are known as the five knowing and working senses. The first are the powers of hearing, feeling, seeing, tasting, and smelling. The latter are the powers of speech, procreation, elimination, grasping, and locomotion. The Samkhya philosophy develops these concepts.

12) *Hatha Yoga Pradipika*, ii, 26-8. Compare *Gheranda Samhita*, i. 45–9: "The Vastis described arc of two kinds, viz.: Jala-Vasti (or water Vasti) and Suska Vasti (or dry Vasti). Water Vasti is done in water and dry Vasti always on land. JALA-VASTI: Entering the water up to the navel and assuming the posture called Utkatasana, let him contract and dilate the sphincter-muscle of the anus. This is called Jala-Vasti. This cures Prameha (urinary disorders), udavarta (disorders of digestion) and Kruravayu (disorders of the wind). The body becomes free from all diseases and becomes as beautiful as that of the god Cupid. STHALA-VASTI: Assuming the posture called Pascimottana, let him move the intestines slowly downwards, then contract and dilate the sphincter-muscle of the anus with Asvini-Mudra. By this practice of Yoga, constipation never occurs, and it increases gastric fire and cures flatulence." These practices are not mentioned in Siva Samhita.

13) See below, p. 45–46 for nauli and p. 76 for asvini mudra.

knees. The purpose of this is to enable one to put forth the necessary muscular effort; so shift around until a comfortable position is found. While in this position, empty the lungs and force the rectum out as far as possible, then draw it in. This requires strong muscular action. Once it is in, while one is still in the original position and holding the breath, do nauli, which isolates the recti muscles of the abdomen. If the action is strong enough, the anal sphincters will open and the water will rush in. By this time the breath will be gone and it will be necessary to rest for a moment. The next time it will not be necessary to force the rectum out; it will be sufficient to draw it in and do nauli. Success is solely dependent upon perfection of nauli and asvini mudra. I was not given the technique of basti until I had perfected the practices of nauli and asvini, which will be discussed later. Because of this I was able to succeed after two or three experiments, which were necessary to find out what the instructions meant. If one is unable to achieve success after executing all the movements, the sphincters may be opened by the fingers, which should be removed the moment the water begins to rush in.

This should be practised upon arising in the morning, before anything has been put into the stomach. It is not essential to have a large quantity of water. It can be done with a very small quantity. On many occasions it has not been necessary for me to use more than a small basin of water. In these instances I experienced no unusual difficulty, except that a little more effort was required to suck in the water. After the colon is filled with water, by isolating the recti muscles and rolling them from left to right it is possible to move the water through the large intestine. When it is time to remove the water, the muscles should be rolled from right to left. It is also helpful to roll the abdomen from the top downward; this will help to squeeze out what remains. I found that if any further trouble is encountered in getting the water out, by using mayurasana[14] it is possible to flush the colon thoroughly. For this purpose the legs should be spread apart, and the posture should be held for at least thirty seconds, after which mayurasana can be repeated if it is still necessary.

The advantages of this practice are self-evident. I found it expedient to include it as part of my daily routine in order to assure a clean

---

14)   This posture has already been described on p. 23 *n*.

intestinal tract. There is not a great deal of waste matter when the diet is so materially reduced; however, it is necessary to keep the system free from the small deposits of waste matter formed by the normal metabolic function of the system. I found basti completely satisfactory for this purpose. Any one living in a modern city may have some doubt as to the practicality of this exercise, in the light of modern methods of colonic irrigation. But it must be kept in mind that these practices were devised centuries before the birth of this western civilization and that they were intended to be used by those living in a very primitive material environment. The Yogi usually carried on his practices in a small cave or in an isolated retreat in the jungle. There were no conveniences; there was nothing but a stream of water and the need to cleanse the system internally. After one has mastered the technique, it will be difficult for him to conceive of a more convenient method.

Neti is given as the next cleansing practice. The description is simple:

A cord made of threads, soft and about six inches long, should be passed through the passage of the nose and taken out by the mouth. This is called by Adepts the Neti Karma. The Neti is the cleaner of the brain and the giver of divine sight. It soon destroys all the diseases of the cervical and scapular regions.[15]

The simplest way I found to do this was to purchase a small catheter—the smallest size. Tip the head back a little and insert the catheter straight into the nose, keeping it as much on a level as possible. Do not be rough, but push it slowly so that there is time enough for the delicate mucous membranes to accommodate themselves. Soon the end will be felt where the nose joins the throat. All that need be done then is to reach into the mouth with the fingers and pull the catheter out. If there is any trouble catching hold of the catheter, coughing a little will help throw it out where it can be reached. When both ends of the catheter are in your hand, draw it back and forth a few times before withdrawing it out through the mouth. This causes the saliva to flow freely and stimulates the entire sinus region.

A substitute that I learned for this technique is to draw water

---

15) *Hatha Yoga Pradipika*, ii, 29–30. Compare *Gheranda Samhita*, i, 50–1: "Take a thin thread, measuring half a cubit and insert it into the nostrils, and passing it through, pull it out by the mouth. This is called Neti-Kriya. By practising the Neti-Kriya, one obtains Khecari Siddhi. It destroys the disorders of phlegm and produces clairvoyance or clear sight."

into the nose and expel it through the mouth and then reverse the process by taking water into the mouth and expelling it through the nose.[16] This last procedure is much more difficult and will require a little experimentation on the part of the student; however, it is not too difficult.

Take a mouthful of water and hold it in the back of the throat without swallowing; close the mouth and shove the tongue against the roof of the mouth, creating a pressure and leaving no way of escape for the water but through the nose. At the same time bend the head forward and blow air out through the nose. One should learn to do this after practising a few times each day for a week. The first few efforts will be handicapped by strange sensations, but these will pass quickly. There is no danger, and the rewards are well worth the effort of learning. I have found this an excellent method of cleansing the head in order to stave off a cold. This technique is not essential in order to qualify for the practice of Yoga; however, it is well worth knowing.

The next practice given to me is the foundation for all advanced work and should be mastered by the student. It is called uddiyana. In the texts it is listed as a mudra; however, it should be perfected as soon as possible.

Uddiyana is so called by the Yogis because by its practice the Prana (Vayu-breath)

---

16) These two methods are not mentioned in *Hatha Yoga Pradipika*. *Gheranda Samhita* describes them as forms of kapalabhati; see i, 55–60: "The Kapalabhati is of three kinds: Vama-krama, Vyut-krama, and Sitkrama. [Krama means performance, method or course of conduct; Vama means left; Vyut, inverted procedure; Sit, hissing sound.] They destroy disorders of phlegm. VAMA-KRAMA: Draw the wind through the left nostril and expel it through the right, and draw it again through the right and expel it through the left. This inspiration and expiration must be done without any force. This practice destroys disorders due to phlegm. VYUT-KRAMA: Draw the water through the two nostrils and expel it through the mouth slowly and slowly. This is called Vyut-krama which destroys disorders due to phlegm. SIT-KRAMA: Suck water through the mouth and expel it through the nostrils. By this practice of Yoga one becomes like the god Cupid. Old age never comes to him and decrepitude never disfigures him. The body becomes healthy, elastic, and disorders due to phlegm arc destroyed."

A similar practice is listed as a mudra. Compare *Gheranda Samhita*, iii, 88–91: "Stand in neck-deep water, draw in the water through the nostrils and throw it out by the mouth. Then draw in the water through (the mouth and expel it through) the nostrils. Let one repeat this again and again. This is called Matangini Mudra (Elephant-mudra), destroyer of decay and death. In a solitary place, free from human intrusion, one should practise with fixed attention this Elephant-mudra; by so doing, he becomes strong like the elephant. Wherever he may be, by this process the Yogin enjoys great pleasure; therefore, this mudra should be practised with great care."

flies (flows) in the Susumna.[17] Uddiyana [means flying up, soaring] is so called because the great bird Prana [breath], tied to it, flies without being fatigued. It is explained below. The belly above the navel is pressed backwards towards the spine. This Uddiyana Bandha is like a lion for the elephant of death. Uddiyana is always very easy when learned from a guru. The practiser of this, if old, becomes young again. The portions above and below the navel, should be drawn backwards towards the spine. By practising this for six months one can undoubtedly conquer death.[18] Of all the Bandhas, Uddiyana is the best; for by binding it firmly liberation comes spontaneously.[19]

A more detailed description will make it easier to learn. Stand with the feet apart and the hands on the bent legs, in a semi-squatting position. Make the posture comfortable, and then empty the lungs. With the breath out, forcibly contract the abdominal muscles, raising the viscera until a large depression is made under the diaphragm (see Plate XXXII).[20] One should be able to place both fists in the pocket that is made. Then suddenly relax. Repeat this alternating contraction and relaxation ten times before taking another breath. This is called one round of ten counts. Before the next round, stand up straight and rest for a few seconds until the normal flow of breath returns. Never

---

17) The channel in the spinal column through which the breath of life is believed to pass.

18) To understand what is meant by a statement of this kind, the student is advised to study *The Tibetan Book of the Dead*, by W. Y. Evans-Wentz.

19) *Hatha Yoga Pradipika*, iii, 54–9. Compare *Gheranda Samhita*, iii, 10–11: "Contract the bowels equally above and below the navel towards the back, so that the abdominal viscera may touch the back. He who practices this Uddiyana (Flying up), without ceasing, conquers death. [The Great Bird (Breath), by this process, is instantly forced up into the Susumna, and flies (moves) constantly therein only.] Of all Bandhas this is the best. The complete practice of this makes emancipation easy."

Compare *Siva Samhita*, IV, 48–52: "When the intestines above and below the navel are brought to the left side, it is called Uddana-Bandha the destroyer of all sins and sorrows. The left side viscera of the abdominal cavity should be brought above the navel. This is Uddana-Bandha, the lion or the elephant of death. The Yogi, who always practises it four times a day, purifies thereby his navel, through which the winds are purified. By practising it for six months, the Yogi certainly conquers death; the gastric fire is kindled, and there takes place an increase of the fluids of the body. Through this, consequently, the Vigrahasiddhi (power of expansion) is also obtained. All the diseases of the Yogi are certainly destroyed by it. Having learnt the method from the Guru, the wise Yogi should practise it with great care. The most inaccessible Mudra should be practised in a retired and undisturbed place."

20) A supplementary practice frequently used to enable one to develop this position is listed in *Gheranda Samhita*, iii, 61: "Make the abdomen look quite hollow just like a tank. This is Tadagi (Tank) Mudra, destroyer of decay and death."

force any exercise or impose a strain upon the system. If this exercise causes undue fatigue, cut the time in half. The practices of Yoga are designed to make one grow strong, and this requires time. When you have rested, empty the lungs and repeat the process another ten times. The average individual should be able to do five rounds; however, if any pain is felt or breathing becomes difficult, begin with three. After a week's time add another five rounds. Naturally, this will vary for each individual, depending on his age, his physical structure, and his condition at the time of starting the practice. After one has a measure of his capacity and has accustomed the body to the exercise, it is possible to increase the number of strokes for each exhalation. However, do not sacrifice the vigour of contraction for speed, which will come in due time.

An outline of the general plan I followed when developing this practice will be a helpful guide: however, it is not intended as final. Each individual must work out his own procedure. It was not long before I could execute twenty contractions on each exhalation for ten rounds. I kept up this pace for one month. After my muscles became hard I practised every morning and late in the afternoon, before dinner. After another month I added five rounds each week to my daily schedule, continuing to repeat it twice a day. When I reached a total of 500 contractions for each practice, I used this standard for a month before I began to add more rounds. My next goal was 750 contractions. This is considered the minimum limit when practising Yoga.

When all signs of effort had gone and I felt as fresh at the end of my practice period as I did at the beginning, I increased the number of contractions on each breath until I was finally able to contract fifty times on one exhalation. I reached this limit by slow stages; at no time did I force the practice. It was not long before I could execute 1,000 contractions twice a day. After another thirty days at this pace I dropped the afternoon practice period and increased the total number of counts in the morning, until I reached a maximum of 1,500 counts.

The entire practice required from thirty to forty minutes, depending upon the length of the intervals between rounds. Nothing is gained by increasing the number of contractions on each breath. It is only a convenience; do not sacrifice thoroughness for speed. I was instructed to build up to this point of efficiency slowly and then to

maintain it for a period of three months. Then the practice is considered mastered; thereafter one is privileged to use it as one sees fit or as
circumstances demand. For ordinary purposes in daily life one or two
hundred contractions are sufficient, but the student whose goal is more
highly developed practices of Yoga should start at the very beginning
to master this technique. It is an important stepping stone.

The next step in my practice was nauli.[21] Any student who has
given six months to uddiyana is ready to attempt this step. It consists of
the isolation and rolling of the rectus abdominis, the straight muscles
of the abdomen. Assume the same semi-squatting position used in uddiyana, but instead of placing the hands far down on the thighs, raise
them a little and turn the arms so that the fingers are on the inside
of the leg rather than on the outside as in the other position. This
enables one to get a better leverage. Empty the lungs and contract all
the muscles of the abdominal area. While holding this position, isolate
the muscles and push them forward (see Plate XXXIV). The student
will have to experiment with various ways of getting control of these
muscles; however, before starting, it is of paramount importance that
he attain a fair degree of efficiency with uddiyana. Only then will it be
easy for him. If nauli seems hopeless at first, do not despair; return to
uddiyana, and the other will come in time.

After the muscles have been isolated so that it is possible to push
them straight forward and draw them back, the student should try
to manipulate each one separately. This is accomplished by bending
slightly to the left and relaxing the muscle on the right side. When in
this position it is possible to work the muscle on the left side independ-
ently of the other (see Plate XXXV). The reverse of this should also
be practised (see Plate XXXVI). The next step is to roll the muscles
from one side to the other. Start by slowly rolling them from left to

---

21) *Compare Hatha Yoga Pradipika*, ii, 33–4: "Sitting on the toes with the heels raised above
the ground, and the palms resting on the ground, in this bent posture the belly is moved forcibly
from left to right just as in vomiting. This is called by adepts the Nauli Karma. It removes dyspepsia, increases appetite and digestion, and is like the goddess of creation and causes happiness. It
dries up all the disorders. This Nauli is an excellent exercise in Hatha Yoga." Instead of this practice,
Gheranda Samhita, i, 52, gives another practice: "With great force move the stomach and intestines
from one side to the other. This is called Lauliki-Yoga. This destroys all diseases and increases the
bodily fire." I was taught lauliki as given here. It can be used by individuals who are physically unable
to learn nauli as I have described it. There are times when lauliki is quite satisfactory, but the student
should endeavour to master nauli, which is one of the fundamental requirements for those who
wish to proceed to the more advanced practices.

right. This should be done ten times on one breath and is called one round of ten counts. Resume natural breathing for a few seconds, then reverse the process by rolling them from right to left ten times. Nothing remains but to build up the strength of the muscles.

This practice requires considerably more power than uddiyana, but by regulated discipline it can be built up to the same number of repetitions in a year's time. I started by working the muscles backward and forward ten times on one breath. After resting I worked the muscle on the left side ten times. After another breath I began on the right muscle. At the end of my first year's work on uddiyana I added ten rounds of each of these movements to my daily schedule for several months.

When I finally became proficient enough so that there was no labour in the practice, I dropped uddiyana and concentrated upon nauli. First I increased the count from ten to twenty-five for each exhalation. When several months had passed, I had a fair degree of control, and I took up the rolling movements. On one exhalation I would roll the recti twenty-five times to the left. After resting a few seconds I rolled the recti twenty-five times to the right. The full practice consisted of ten rounds each—forward, to the left, and to the right—or 250 straight forward, then 250 times to the left and 250 times to the right. As the months went by I continued to increase the number of rounds, but never the number of movements on each expulsion of air. For maximum efficiency twenty-five counts was most satisfactory. It is not necessary to carry these exercises to such extremes in order to obtain physical benefits. They were assigned to me as a preparation for the advanced practice of Yoga, and I had to master them before I was permitted to take up the next step. During this initial period, when I was learning techniques, I noted a sharper appetite, better vision, and better physical tone. All the muscles of my body were in good condition, hard and solid. I enjoyed excellent health and was free from all minor ailments of sedentary life.

The last purification practice given to me was bhastrika (bellows), which is listed as a breathing exercise in the text. The description given in the text is rather vague, considering its importance:

The Padmasana consists in crossing the legs and placing the feet on both the thighs; it is the destroyer of all sins. Binding the Padmasana and keeping the body straight, closing the mouth carefully, let the air be expelled through the nose. It should be filled up to the lotus of the heart, by drawing it in with force, making noise and touching the throat, the chest and the head. It should be expelled again and filled again and again as before, just as a pair of bellows of the blacksmith is worked with force. In the same way the air of the body should be moved intelligently, filling it through the right nostril when fatigue is experienced. The nose should be lightly held with the middle and forefingers, till the belly is filled with air and does not become heavy. Having confined it properly, it should be expelled through the Ida (left nostril). This destroys Vata, pitta (bile) and phlegm[22] and increases the digestive power (the gastric fire). The air so treated quickly awakens the Kundalini,[23] purifies the system, gives pleasure, and is beneficial. It destroys phlegm and the impurities accumulated at the entrance of the Brahma Nadi. This Bhastrika should be performed plentifully for it breaks the three knots; Brahma granthi (in the chest), Visnu granthi (in the throat) and Rudra granthi[24](between the eyebrows) of the body.[25]

The technique is quite simple. Assume one of the meditation asanas—preferably padmasana, but siddhasana will do in the beginning. When the position is comfortable, force all the air out of the lungs by a sudden contraction of the abdominal muscles. Automatically they will return to their natural position; so there is no need of any conscious

22)   These are the three basic principles of the system of physiology upon which Hatha Yoga is based.

23)   This is the latent creative force in man. See below, p. 68.

24)   It is said that when the latent creative force of man becomes dynamic and begins to move through its channel in the spinal cord, at certain places, where there is a nerve ganglion, it encounters difficulties. This would be analogous to a point where a number of electric wires converge before being distributed. There are special techniques for overcoming these obstacles.

25)   *Hatha Yoga Pradipika*, ii, 59-67. Compare *Gheranda Samhita*, v, 75–7: "As the bellows of the ironsmith constantly dilate and contract, similarly let him slowly draw in the air by both nostril and expand the stomach; then throw it out quickly (the wind making sound like bellows). Having thus inspired and expired quickly twenty times, let him perform Kumbhaka; then let him expel it by the previous method. Let the wise one perform this Bhastrika (bellows-like) Kumbhaka thrice: he will never suffer from any disease and will be always healthy."

Compare this with the description of the last purification process given in the text called kapalabhati. *Hatha Yoga Pradipika*, ii, 35–7: "When inhalation and exhalation are performed very quickly, like a pair of bellows of a blacksmith, it dries up all the disorders from the excess of phlegm, and is known as Kapala Bhati. When Pranayama is performed after getting rid of obesity born of the defects of phlegm, by the performance of the six duties, it easily brings success. Some acharyas (teachers) do not advocate any other practice, being of opinion that all the impurities are dried up by the practice of Pranayama alone." For a description of kapalabhati as given in *Gheranda Samhita*, see above, p. 41 *n. The* descriptions given by the two texts differ, but this is of no practical import. The purpose of this practice can be seen from the meaning of the word. In Sanskrit 'kapala' means 'skull' and 'bhati" is derived from the root meaning 'to shine'.

effort for the inhalation. This forced exhalation and automatic inhalation should be done at the rate of sixty times a minute for one minute and should be followed by a short suspension. Afterward let the air out slowly and when the lungs are empty resume normal breathing for a minute; then repeat the process. For ordinary purposes this can be done from three to five times. If the individual has perfected uddiyana and nauli, this rate for one minute will be an easy routine. I began this way, but in a couple of weeks I increased the speed of the exhalations to 120 a minute and extended the time to two minutes. I found no difficulty in suspending for two minutes. In three weeks I was able to perform ten rounds without the slightest discomfort. After another month I increased the breathing time to three minutes and decreased the rest period, but did not alter the suspension. I found this sufficient for all practical purposes, for I was using the exercise as a means of cleansing the system.

With no practice of Yoga should pain be endured. Pain is treated by the Yogis as a stop signal. Until the muscles are hardened, the student may feel a 'stitch' in his side. When this happens, rest for a few moments and then start again. If it persists, wait until the following day.

These are the basic purification processes, and without them progress is hampered; but with them success is readily forthcoming. Their general effect seems to be better health and the normal mental conditions that accompany such a state of well-being.

PRANAYAMA

A CCORDING to Patanjali "Pranayama is the cessation of the inspiratory and expiratory movements of breath which follows when that has been secured; thence the cover of light is destroyed and the mind becomes fit for concentration."[1] Vachaspati says, "Pranayama renders the mind fit for concentration, by making it steady."[2]

Our text opens its chapter on pranayama as follows:

Posture being established, a Yogi, master of himself, eating salutary and moderate food, should practise pranayama, as instructed by his guru. When Prana (the life breath) moves, the mind also moves. When Prana ceases to move, the mind becomes motionless. (The body of) the Yogi becomes stiff as a stump. Therefore, one should control Prana. So long as the (breathing) air stays in the body, so long is life. Death consists in the passing out of the (breathing) air. It is, therefore, necessary to restrain the breath. The breath does not pass through the middle channel (susumna), owing to the impurities of the nadis. How then can success be attained, and how can there be the unmani avastha [mindlessness].[3]

All texts agree that pranayama is impossible until the nerve channels (nadis) are thoroughly cleansed.

When the whole system of nadis which is full of impurities, is cleaned, then the Yogi becomes able to conserve the Prana (breath). Therefore, Pranayama should be performed daily with sattvika buddhi (intellect free from rajas and tamas or activity and sloth), in order to drive out the impurities of the susumna.[4]

---

1) *The Yoga Sutra of Patanjali*, ii, 49, 52, 53.

2) *Ibid.*, Vachaspati's gloss, ii, 104.

3) *Hatha Yoga Pradipika*, ii, 1–4.

4) *Ibid.*, 5–6. Compare the opening section on 'Purification of Nadis' in *Gheranda Samhita*, v, 33–5: "He should sit on a seat of Kusa-grass, or an antelope skin, or tiger skin or a blanket, or on earth, calmly and quietly, facing east or north. Having purified the nadis, let him begin Pranayama. Candakapali said. 'Ocean of mercy! How are nadis purified, what is the purification of Nadis; I want to learn all this; recite to me.' Gheranda said, 'The Vayu does not (cannot) enter the nadis so long as they are full of impurities. How then can Pranayama be accomplished? How can there be knowledge of Tattvas? Therefore, first the Nadis should be purified, and then Pranayama should be practised.'"

The generally accepted method for purification of the nadis by breathing is then given.

Sitting in the Padmasana posture the Yogi should fill in the air through the left nostril (closing the right one); and keeping it confined according to one's ability, it should be expelled slowly through the right nostril. Then, drawing in the air through the right nostril slowly, the belly should be filled, and after performing Kumbhaka [suspension] as before, it should be expelled slowly through the left nostril. Inhaling thus through the one, through which it was expelled, and having restrained it till possible, it should be exhaled through the other, slowly and not forcibly. If the air be inhaled through the left nostril, it should be expelled again through the other, and filling it through the right nostril, and confining it should be expelled through the left nostril. By practising in this way, through the right and the left nostrils alternately, the whole of the collection of the nadis of the yamis (practisers) becomes clean, i.e. free from impurities, after three months.[5]

This process of alternate breathing is the accepted traditional technique and is by far the most satisfactory. I have been taught several

---

5) *Hatha Yoga Pradipika*, 7–10. Compare *Gheranda Samhita*, v, 38–45: "Sitting in the Padma-sana posture, and performing the adoration of the Guru, etc., as taught by the Teacher, let him perform purification of Nadis for success in Pranayama. Contemplating on Vayu-Bija (yam) [the seed syllable of the energy of air], full of energy and of a smoke-colour, let him draw in breath by the left nostril, repeating the Bija sixteen times. This is Puraka. Let him restrain the breath for a period of sixty-four repetitions of the Mantra. This is Kumbhaka. Then let him expel the air by the right nostril slowly during a period occupied by repeating the Mantra thirty-two times. The root of the navel is the seat of Agni-Tattva [Fire-essence]. Raising the fire from that place, join the Prthivi-Tattva [Earth-essence] with it; then contemplate on this mixed light. Then repeating sixteen times the Agni-Bija (ram) [The seed syllable of the energy of fire] let him draw in breath by the right nostril, and retain it for the period of sixty-four repetitions of the Mantra, and then expel it by the left nostril for a period of thirty-two repetitions of the Mantra. Then fixing the gaze on the tip of the nose and contemplat-ing the luminous reflection of the moon there, let him inhale through the left nostril, repeating the Bija tham sixteen times; let him retain it by repeating the Bija tham sixty-four times; in the meanwhile imagine (or contemplate) that the nectar flowing from the moon at the tip of the nose runs through all the vessels of the body, and purifies them. Thus contemplating, let him exhale repeating thirty-two times the Prthivi Bija lam [the seed syllable of the energy of earth]. By these three Pranayamas the nadis are purified. Then sitting firmly in a posture, let him begin regular Pranayama." This would be true only in the event that one is already a Yogi. For others a much longer period is obviously needed.

Compare *Siva Samhita*, iii, 22–4: "Then let the wise practitioner close with his right thumb the Pingala (the right nostril), inspire air through the Ida (the left nostril); and keep air confined—sus-pend his breathing—as long as he can, and afterwards let him breathe out slowly, and not forcibly, through the right nostril. Again, let him draw breath through the right nostril, and stop breathing as long as his strength permits; then let him expel the air through the left nostril, not forcibly but slowly and gently. According to the above method of Yoga, let him practise twenty kumbhakas (stopping of the breath). He should practise this daily without neglect or idleness, and free from all duels (of love and hatred, and doubt and contention), etc."

varieties, but none of them is of such outstanding importance that it should be recommended for practice. I was directed to use bhastrika to purify the nadis; however, those who are unable to develop bhastrika, as I have described it, can use this standard method of alternate breathing.

In the traditional manner, the subject of regular pranayama is introduced as follows:

Brahma and other Devas were always engaged in the exercise of Pranayama, and, by means of it, got rid of the fear of death. Therefore, one should practise Pranayama regularly. So long as the breath is restrained in the body, so long as the mind is undisturbed, and so long as the gaze is fixed between the eyebrows, there is no fear from Death. When the system of Nadis becomes clear of the impurities by properly controlling the prana, then the air, piercing the entrance of the Susumna, enters it easily. Steadiness of mind comes when the air moves freely in the middle (Susumna). That is the manonmani condition, which is attained when the mind becomes calm. To accomplish it, various Kumbhakas are performed by those who are expert in the methods; for, by the practice of different Kumbhakas, wonderful success is attained. Kumbhakas are of eight kinds, viz. Surya Bhedana, Ujjayi, Sitkari, Sitali, Bhastrika, Bhramari, Murchha, and Plavini.[6]

These are the fundamental breathing practices used to suspend the flow of breath and to conquer the mind according to Yogic tradition. The inherent danger of any such undertaking is self-apparent; therefore the individual investigator is advised to take every precaution.[7] Each practice has its own individual purpose. Though it is not necessary to

---

6) *Hatha Yoga Pradipika*, ii, 39–44. Compare *Gheranda Samhita*, v, 46: "The Kumbhakas or retentions of breath are of eight sorts; Sahita, Surya-bheda, Ujjayi, Sitali, Bhastrika, Bhramari, Murchha, and Kevali." The variations will be discussed in their proper sequence.

7) *Hatha Yoga Pradipika*, ii, 15–20: "Just as lions, elephants and tigers are controlled by and by, so the breath is controlled by slow degrees, otherwise (i.e., by being hasty or using too much force) it kills the practiser himself. When Pranayama, etc. are performed properly, they eradicate all diseases, but an improper practice generates diseases. Hiccup, asthma, cough, pain in the head, the ears, and the eyes; these and other various kinds of diseases are generated by the disturbances of the breath. The air should be expelled with proper tact, and should be filled in skilfully, and should be kept confined properly. Thus it brings success. When the nadis become free from impurities, and there appear the outward signs of success, such as lean body and glowing colour, then one should feel certain of success. By removing the impurities of the nadis the air can be restrained, according to one's wish, and the appetite is increased, the divine sound is awakened, and the body becomes healthy."
   Compare *Siva Samhita*, iii, 31: "The following qualities are surely always found in the body of every Yogi:—Strong appetite, good digestion, cheerfulness, handsome figure, great courage, mighty enthusiasm and full strength."

use them all, I learned all and shall discuss each in the order in which I was instructed—the order most helpful to my progress.

The first is surya bhedana (piercing the solar discus). The technique is simple:

Taking any comfortable posture and performing the asana, the Yogi should draw in the air slowly, through the right nostril. Then it should be confined within, so that it fills from the nails [of the toes] to the tips of the hair [on the head], and then let out through the left nostril slowly.[8]

––––––––––––––––––

8) *Hatha Yoga Pradipika,* ii, 48–9. For the effect this practice is supposed to have on the body (see 50): "This excellent Surya Bhedana cleanses the forehead (frontal sinuses) destroys the disorders of Vata and removes the worms, and, therefore, it should be performed again and again." Compare *Gheranda Samhita*, v. 58–68: "Inspire with all your strength the external air through the sun-tube (right nostril): retain this air with the greatest care, performing the Jalandhara Mudra. Let the Kumbhaka be kept up until the perspiration burst out from the tips of the nails and the roots of the hair.

"The Vayus are ten, namely, Prana, Apana, Samana, Udana, and Vyana; Naga, Kurma, Krkara, Devadatta, and Dhanamjaya."

"The Prana moves always in the heart; the Apana in the sphere of anus; the Samana in the navel region; the Udana in the throat; and the Vyana pervades the whole body. These are the five principal Vayus, known as Pranadi. They belong to the inner body. The Nagadi five Vayus belong to the Outer body.

"I now tell thee the seats of these five external Vayus. The Naga-Vayu performs the function of belching; the Kurma opens the eye-lids; the Krkara causes sneezing; the Devadatta does yawning; the Dhanamjaya pervades the whole gross body, and does not leave it even after death.

"The Naga -Vayu gives rise to consciousness, the Kurma causes vision, the Krkara hunger and thirst, the Devadatta produces yawning and by Dhanamjaya sound is produced. This does not leave the body ever for a minute.

"Let him raise all these Vayus, which are separated by the Suryanadi, from the root of the navel; then exhale by the Ida-nadi, slowly with confidence and with unbroken, continuous force. Let him again inhale through the right nostril, retaining it, as taught above, and exhale it again. Let him do this again and again. (In this process, the air is always inspired through the Surya-nadi.)

"Surya-bheda Kumbhaka destroys decay and death, awakens the Kundali Sakti, increases the bodily fire, O Canda! thus have I taught thee the Suryabhedana Kumbhaka."

For a comparative description of the Vayus see *Siva Samhita*, iii. 1–9: "In the heart, there is a brilliant lotus with twelve petals adorned with brilliant signs. It has the letters from k to th (i.e. k, kh, g, gh, n, ch, chh, j, jh, n, t, th), the twelve beautiful letters. The Prana lives there, adorned with various desires, accompanied by its past works, that have no beginning, and joined with egoism (Ahankara). From the different modification of the Prana, it receives various names; all of them cannot be stated here. Prana, Apana, Samana, Udana, Vyana, Naga, Kurma, Krikara, Devatta, and Dhananjaya. These are the ten principal names, described by me in this Sastra; they perform all the functions, incited thereto by their own actions. Again, out of these ten, the first five are the leading ones; even among these, the Prana and Apana are the highest agents in my opinion. The seat of the Prana is the heart; of the Apana, the anus; of the Samana the region around the navel; of the Udana the throat; while the Vyana moves all over the body. The five remaining Vayus, the Naga, etc., perform the following functions in the body; Eructation, opening the eyes, hunger and thirst, gaping or yawning, and lastly hiccup. He who in this way knows the microcosm of the body, being absolved from all sins, reaches the highest state."

A general description of the supplementary disciplines that I was taught by my teacher will be helpful. This particular practice derives its name from the fact that the inhalation is always through the right nostril. It may be performed in any cross-legged posture that is comfortable; however, padmasana is the required posture for the last stages of pranayama. For the most part I used siddhasana, and I encountered no special difficulty. Inhale to full capacity through the right nostril, swallow, suspend, and then bury the chin in the jugular notch. This last act is called jalandhara mudra (chin lock)[9] and should be used whenever the breath is suspended. During suspension, contract the muscles of the abdominal area as in uddiyana. These acts help to lock the air within the body and create an abdominal pressure. The purpose assigned to this pressure is that it enables one ultimately to control the breath at will and thus to gain control of the mind. However, I was advised never to hold the breath so long that it caused undue strain. It is the repetition of the practice that is recommended, not the use of a great amount of effort.

One round of this practice consists of a deep inhalation through the right nostril, a suspension, and an exhalation through the left nostril. Start the next round immediately, without a pause, by inhaling through the right nostril and suspending as before. The length of the suspension will vary in each individual case. I started with thirty seconds which is considered a good measure for the average beginner. Ten rounds was my first standard. When I could do this without any discomfort, I increased the total number of rounds by units of five rounds until the maximum of eighty was reached. It is important that the process be continuous, with the breath under constant control. Eventually this method of breathing becomes as natural as normal breathing. I was instructed that in all breathing practices it is paramount that the breath never be allowed to escape rapidly. I judiciously heeded every word of advice, and therefore cannot report what ill effects might result from letting the breath burst out.

When I first began to practise the breathing exercises I did them every morning and every evening. Later I introduced another practice

---

9)   This is a simple technique used to prevent the air from rushing up into the head. For classical description see below, pp. 77-78.

period at noon, and finally one at midnight.[10] However, this is quite unnecessary for the beginner. I was warned never to practise until exhausted. In accordance with instructions, I rested afterward for some thirty minutes before engaging in any vigorous action or eating heavy food. This is to permit the body to adjust itself. After finishing it was my practice to sip a small glass of milk. This I found to be most satisfying, as well as strengthening.

There is a traditional technique used for closing the nostrils.[11] Press the first finger and the middle finger against the palm and use the thumb to close one nostril and the ring finger and the little finger to close the other nostril. When both nostrils are open, the fingers may rest on the bridge of the nose. When it is not necessary to regulate the flow of the breath from one nostril to the other, it is customary to place the hands in the lap, letting one hand rest in the palm of the other. Another way is to join the tip of the thumb and the tip of the first finger and let the back of the wrists rest on the respective knees with the fingers extended.

The description in the text of the next practice, called ujjayi (victorious) is simple.

Having closed the mouth the air should be drawn again and again through the nostrils in such a way that it goes touching from the throat to the chest, and making noise while passing. It should be restrained, as before, and then let out through Ida (the left nostril). This removes slesma (phlegm) in the throat and increases the appetite. It destroys the defects of the nadis, dropsy and disorders of Dhatu (humours). Ujjayi should be performed in all conditions of life, even while walking or sitting.[12]

---

10) See *Hatha Yoga Pradipika*, ii, II: "Kumbhakas should be performed gradually four times during day and night (i.e. morning, noon, evening and midnight), till the number of Kumbhakas for one time is 80 and for the day and night together it is 320." Compare *Siva Samhita*, iii, 25: "These Kumbhakas should be practised four times: once (I) early in the morning at sunrise, (2) then at midday, (3) the third time at sunset, and (4) the fourth time at midnight." This is the accepted discipline for any breathing practice; however, three periods, or even two, are sufficient in the beginning.

11) *Gheranda Samhita*, v, 53: "Let him practise, thus alternating the nostrils again and again. When inhalation is completed, close both nostrils, the right one by the thumb and the left one by the ring-finger and little-finger, never using the index and middle fingers. This nostril is to be closed so long as Kumbhaka is.

12) *Hatha Yoga Pradipika*, ii, 51–3. Compare Gheranda Samhita, v, 69–72: "Close the mouth, draw in the external air by both the nostrils, and pull the internal air from the lungs and throat; retain them in the mouth. Then having washed the mouth (i.e. expelled the air through mouth) perform Jalandhara. Let him perform Kumbhaka with all his might and retain the air unhindered. All works

This is an easy method of deep-chest breathing with a slightly closed glottis. Any posture suitable for pranayama is allowed. It may be practised in almost any condition of life, while standing, sitting, or even walking; however, I have never had occasion to test it in any posture but the postures of meditation. I was taught to wash the tongue and mouth before starting the practice. The technique is accomplished by inhaling in such a manner that a soft sobbing sound of uniform pitch is made. After the suspension, swallow, do Jalandhara, and suspend. While holding the breath, elevate the chest and contract the muscles of the abdominal walls as in the practice just described. The text advises to exhale through the left nostril; however, I was permitted to exhale through both nostrils, making a sound similar to the one made during the inhalation. The abdominal muscles should be contracted until the last vestige of air has been removed from the lungs. The exhalation should be twice the length of the inhalation, but it should not be prolonged until it is impossible to proceed immediately to the next inhalation without snatching a few extra breaths. Each step must be regulated so that a process of rhythmic breathing is established. To prepare for this practice it is permissible to omit the suspension for the first week or so and develop control of the inhalation and exhalation. I started with four rounds a minute and was able to establish control within a week.

The next two practices should be described together.

Sitkari [hissing sound] is performed by drawing in the air through the mouth, keeping the tongue between the lips. The air thus drawn in should not be expelled through the mouth, but by the nostril. By practising in this way, one becomes next to the God of Love in beauty. He is regarded adorable by the Yoginis [female yogis] and becomes the author and destroyer of the cycle of creation. He is not afflicted with hunger, thirst, sleep, or lassitude. The Sattva of his body becomes free from all the disturbances. In truth, he becomes the lord of the Yogis in this world.[13]

The next technique follows:

As in the above (Sitkari), the tongue to be protruded a little out of the lips, when

---

are accomplished by Ujjayi Kumbhaka. He is never attacked by phlegm-diseases, or nerve-diseases, or indigestion, or dysentery, or consumption, or cough; or fever, or (enlarged) spleen. Let a man perform Ujjayi to destroy decay and death."

13) *Hatha Yoga Pradipika* ii, 54–6. This first stage is not listed in the *Gheranda Samhita*.

the air is drawn in. It is kept confined, as before, and then expelled slowly through the nostrils. This Sitali [cooling] Kumbhaka cures colic (enlarged) spleen, fever, disorders of bile, hunger, thirst, and counteracts poisons.[14]

There is little need for special comment on these two methods. They are supposed to be used for cooling the system; however, I have never had occasion to test them for this purpose. The first is done by locking the teeth and suspending the tongue so that it does not touch any part of the mouth. Suck in the air between the teeth, making all the noise possible, and then exhale through the nose without suspending. I was taught two ways of doing Sitali. The first is to turn the tongue back until it touches the soft palate and then inhale, do the chin lock and suspend. The second is to roll the tongue lengthwise into a trough and then protrude it a little beyond the lips. While holding the tongue in this position, draw in the air, perform the chin lock, and suspend. In both instances exhalation should be through the nostrils. No special problem should arise with these two practices.

The next practice is bhastrika,[15] which was discussed above as a purification technique. The remaining kumbhakas listed in the text are bhramari, murchha, and plavini. "Bhramari consists in filling the air with force, which makes a noise like a male bee, and in expelling it slowly which makes a noise like a female bee; this practice causes a sort of ecstasy in the minds of Yogindras."[16] "Closing the passages

14) *Ibid.*, 57–8. Compare *Gheranda Samhita*, v, 73–4: "Draw in the air through the mouth (with the lips contracted and tongue thrown out), and fill the stomach slowly. Retain it there for a short time. Then exhale it through both the nostrils. Let the Yogin always practise this Sitali Kumbhaka, giver of bliss; by so doing he will be free from indigestion, phlegm and bilious disorders."

15) See above, pp. 45–46.

16) See *Hatha Yoga Pradipika*, ii, 68. Compare *Gheranda Samhita*, v. 78–82: "At past midnight in a place where there are no sounds of animals etc., to be heard, let the Yogin practise Puraka and Kumbhaka, closing the ears by the hands. He will then hear various internal sounds in his right ear. The first sound will be like that of crickets, then that of a flute, then that of a beetle, then that of bells, then those of gongs of bell-metal, trumpets, kettle-drums, mrdanga, military drums, and dundubhi, etc. Thus various rounds are cognised by daily practice of this Kumbhaka. Last of all is heard the Ana-hata sound rising from the heart; of this sound there is a resonance, in that resonance there is a Light. In that Light the mind should be immersed. When the mind is absorbed then it reaches the highest seat of Visnu (parama-pada). By success in this Bhramari Kumbhaka one gets success in Samadhi." This practice is frequently called the 'beetle-droning Kumbhaka'. It can be done in any comfortable posture and is best practised at midnight in absolute silence. The sound is accomplished by utter-ing 'Ah' as low in the throat as possible vibrating the palate. Eventually this tone becomes clear. This practise is designed to produce a specific condition in the mind, but this cannot be effected until

with Jalandhara Bandha firmly at the end of Puraka, and expelling the air slowly, is called Murchha, from its causing the mind to swoon and giving comfort."[17] This practice derives its name from the fact that it causes the mind to faint. This is accomplished by locking the air within the body during the suspension and focusing the mind on the space between the eyebrows until it swoons. I was also taught to do this by suspending the breath outside the lungs. The beginner is advised not to work on this practice during his preparatory period. It has a normal place in the more highly developed stages of pranayama when working with the mind. "When the belly is filled with air freely circulating within the body, the body easily floats even in the deepest water like the leaf of a lotus."[18]

This condition obtains only for those who have mastered pranayama in its advanced stages. These are techniques for inducing certain psychological phenomena which are out of place at this time. I was not given these practices until I had fully developed pranayama.

The concluding discussion of the text presents the ultimate aim of all breathing practices.

Considering Puraka (filling),   (expelling) and Kumbhaka (confining), Pranayama is of three kinds. Accompanied by Puraka and Rechaka, and without these, Kum-

---

it is possible to hold the breath for several minutes at a time. Only the most highly developed Yogis experience these various sounds.

17)   See *Hatha Yoga Pradipika,* ii, 69. *Compare Gheranda Samhita,* v, 83: "Having performed Kumbhaka with comfort, let him withdraw the mind from all objects and fix it in the space between the eyebrows. This causes fainting of the mind and gives happiness. For, by this joining the Manas (Mind) with the Atman (Soul), the bliss of Yoga is certainly obtained."

18)   See *Hatha Yoga Pradipika,* ii, 70.

bhaka is of two kinds only, i.e., Sahita[19] (with) and Kevala[20] (alone). Exercise in

19)   Compare *Gheranda Samhita*, v, 47–57: "The Sahita Kumbhaka is of two sorts; Sagarbha and Nigarbha (Sound and Without Sound). The Kumbhaka performed by the repetition of Bija Mantra is Sagarbha; that done without such repetition is Nigarbha. First I shall tell thee the Sagarbha Pranayama. Sitting in Sukhasana posture, facing east or north, let one contemplate on Brahma full of Rajas quality of a blood-red colour, in the form of the letter 'A'. Let the wise practitioner inhale by the left nostril, repeating 'A' sixteen times. Then before he begins retention (but at the end of inhalation), let him perform Uddiyana Bandha. Then let him retain breath by repeating 'U' sixty-four times, contemplating on Hari, of a black colour and Sattva quality. Then let him exhale the breath through the right nostril by repeating makara thirty-two times, contemplating Siva of a white colour and of Tamas quality. Then again inhale through Pingala (right nostril), retain by Kumbhaka, and exhale by Ida (left nostril), in the method taught above, changing the nostrils alternately. Let him practise thus alternating the nostrils again and again. When inhalation is completed, close both nostrils, the right one by the thumb and the left one by the ring-finger and little-finger, never using the index and middle-fingers. The nostrils to be closed as long as Kumbhaka is.

"The Nigarbha (or simple or mantraless) Pranayama is performed without the repetition of Bija mantra; and the period of Puraka (inhalation of inspiration), Kumbhaka (retention), and Rechaka (expiration), may be extended from one to hundred matras, The best is twenty Matras: i.e., Puraka 20 seconds, Kumbhaka 80, and Rechaka 40 seconds. The sixteen matras is middling, i.e. 16, 64, 32. The twelve matras is the lowest, i.e. 12, 48, 24. Thus the Pranayama is of three sorts. By practising the lowest Pranayama for some time, the body begins to quiver (especially there is a feeling of quivering along the spinal cord). By the highest Pranayama one leaves the ground, i.e. there is levitation. These signs attend the success of these three sorts of Pranayama. By Pranayama is attained the power of levitation (Khecari Sakti), by Pranayama diseases are cured, by Pranayama the Sakti (spiritual energy) is awakened, by Pranayama is obtained the calmness of mind and exaltation of mental powers (clairvoyance, etc.); by this, mind becomes full of bliss; verily the practitioner of Pranayama is happy."

20)   Kevali is the eighth kumbhaka listed in *Gheranda Samhita* and is described at length; see v, 84–96: 'The breath of every person in entering makes the sound of 'sah' and in coming out that of 'ham'. These two sounds make (so'ham 'I am He') or (hamsah 'The Great Swan'). Throughout a day and a night there are twenty-one thousand and six hundred such respirations (that is 15 respirations per minute). Every living being (Jiva) performs this japa (repetition) unconsciously, but constantly. This is called Ajapa gayattri. This Ajapa-japa is performed in three places. i.e. in the Muladhara (the space between the anus and membranum virile), in the Anahata lotus (heart) and the Ajna lotus (the space where the nostrils unite). This body is ninety-six digits long (i.e. six feet) as a standard. The ordinary length of the air current when expired is twelve digits (nine inches); in singing its length becomes sixteen digits (one foot); in eating, it is twenty digits (15 inches), in walking, it is twenty-four digits (18 inches); in sleep, it is thirty digits (22½ inches); in copulation it is thirty-six digits (27 inches), and in taking physical exercises, it is more than that. By decreasing the natural length of the expired current from nine inches to less and less, there takes place increase of life; and by increasing the current, there is decrease of life. So long as breath remains in the body there is no death. When the full length of the wind is all confined in the body, nothing being allowed to go out, it is Kevela Kumbhaka.

"All Jivas are constantly and unconsciously reciting this Ajapa Mantra, only for a fixed number of times every day, But a Yogin should recite this consciously and counting the numbers. By doubling the number of Ajapa (i.e. by 30 respirations per minute), the state of Manonmani (fixedness of mind) is attained. There are no regular Rechaka and Puraka in this process. It is only (Kevala) Kumbhaka. By inspiring air by nostrils, let him perform Kevala Kumbhaka. On the first day let him retain breath from one to sixty-four times. This Kevali should he performed eight times a day, once every three hours; or one may do it five times a day, as I shall tell thee. First in the early morning, then at

Sahita should be continued until success in Kevala is gained. This latter is simply confining the air with ease, without Rechaka and Puraka. This unassisted Kumbhaka is Pranayama *par excellence*.[21] When it can be performed successfully without Rechaka and Puraka, there is nothing in the three worlds which may be difficult to obtain. He who is competent to keep the air confined according to pleasure, by means of Kevala Kumbhaka, obtains the position of Raja Yoga undoubtedly. Kundalini awakens by Kumbhaka,[22] and by its awakening Susumna becomes free from impurities and success in Hatha Yoga is accomplished. No success in Raja Yoga without Hatha Yoga, and no success in Hatha Yoga without Raja Yoga.[23] One should, therefore, practise both of these well, till complete success is gained. On the completion of Kumbhaka, the mind should be given rest. By practising in this way one is raised to the position of (succeeds in getting) Raja Yoga.[24]

---

noon, then in the twilight, then at midnight, and then in the fourth quarter of the night. Or one may do it thrice a day, i.e., in the morning, noon and evening. So long as success is not obtained in Kevali, he should increase the length of ajapa-japa every day, one to five times. He who knows Pranayama and Kevali is the real Yogin. What can he not accomplish in this world who has acquired success in Kevali Kumbhaka?"

21)   Compare *Siva Samhita*, iii, 39: "When the Yogi can, of his will, regulate the air and stop the breath (whenever and how long) he likes, then certainly he gets success in Kumbhaka, and from success in Kumbhaka only, what things cannot the Yogi command here?

22)   Kundalini is believed to be the static background against which the phenomena of life are manifest. In order to understand the full implication of this term, which has no Western equivalent, see *Serpent Power*, by Arthur Avalon. It is fully discussed in that volume. The awakening of this latent force which is believed to reside in man is the final aim of all Hatha Yoga. That is why it is frequently called Kundalini Yoga; however, special techniques are needed to effect this result. Compare the statement on "The Awakening of Kundalini," in *Siva Samhita*, iv, 12–14: "Now I shall tell you the best means of attaining success in Yoga. The practitioners should keep it secret. It is the inaccessible Yoga. When the sleeping goddess Kundalini is awakened through the grace of Guru, then all the lotuses (nerve centres) and the bonds are readily pierced through and through. Therefore, in order that the goddess, who is asleep (latent) in the mouth of the Brahmarandhra be awakened, the Mudras should be practised with the greatest care." "Brahmarandhra" is said to be the fontanel.

23)   Compare *Siva Samhita*, v. 181: "The Hatha Yoga cannot be obtained without the Raja Yoga, nor can the Raja Yoga be attained without the Hatha Yoga. Therefore, let the Yogi first learn the Hatha Yoga from the instructions of the wise Guru."

24)   *Hatha Yoga Pradipika*, ii, 71–7. Patanjali mentions only four kinds of pranayama; see the *Yoga Sutras of Patanjali*, ii, 50–l: "Manifestation as external, internal and total restraint is regulated by plan, time, and number; and thus it becomes long in duration and subtle. The fourth is that which follows when the spheres of the external and internal have been passed." By place is meant the duration of these which is called Matra. This is generally considered to be equivalent to our second. Vachaspati in his Gloss on this aphorism says, "A 'matra' (measure) is the time which is taken up by thrice turning up one's hand over one's knee and then snapping the fingers once. Measured by thirty-six such matras is the first attempt (udghata) which is mild. Twice that is the second, which is middling.

Kevala is absolute suspension, the ultimate aim of all breathing practices; however, it is not to be attempted until the body has been thoroughly purified and some degree of control over the flow of breath has been established. I was required to perfect bhastrika to cleanse the system and to use the simple process of alternate breathing for regulating the breath. At various periods I tried all these regulatory processes and observed no marked reactions that would lead me to recommend one in preference to another. They seem to vary more in degree than in value, one imposing less of a strain upon the system than another; so the simpler forms should be used in the beginning.

The technique I finally used was simple. After some fifteen minutes of bhastrika, I began pranayama, which consisted of deep inhalation, suspension for two minutes, and slow exhalation. I was taught to let the breath out twice as slowly as the rate of inhalation. In the beginning the inhalation was ten seconds and the exhalation was twenty seconds. Later I increased it to fifteen seconds for the inspiration and thirty seconds for the expiration. At all times I kept the breath under complete control and did not have a pause to rest or inhale extra air between such rounds. I started with ten rounds, which is an easy standard for anyone in good condition; however, it is not enough to enable one to take up the next stage of Yoga, control of the mind.

After the first week I began to increase my suspension by units of thirty seconds; however, I never added more time until I could execute the standard at hand without the slightest muscular effort and sense of strain. When I had held my breath for a minute or so there was an automatic impulse to start breathing. This was subdued by performing the act of swallowing and exerting greater force on the contracted muscles of the abdomen. At the same time the air would try to force itself out and various singing sounds made themselves felt in my head. I was told never to go beyond this point, for this was the measure of my capacity. Until all these symptoms had passed away and I could remain at perfect ease with breath suspended, I was not allowed to increase the duration of my suspension. In this way all dangers were avoided.

No special difficulty was encountered until I reached a four-minute suspension. I had no trouble in holding my breath for that length of time for a single suspension, but I found that to use it as a standard for

Thrice that is the third, which is intense. This is the Pranayama as measured by number."

ten rounds was a real task. The automatic impulse to breathe became so strong that it was almost impossible for me to subdue it.

At this time I was instructed to begin using khecari mudra. This is a technique of swallowing the tongue which will be discussed later. After this I had no special problem. It was then only a matter of time. I finally developed my capacity so that I could use a five-minute suspension for my ten rounds; however, three minutes can be used. For a single suspension I could hold my breath several minutes longer as a test of my general condition. Still, this is far from the standard required by the texts for attaining the supernatural powers described in all Yogic literature.[25] To acquire such powers it is necessary to hold the breath for an hour or more; it is easy to understand why samadhi is so seldom achieved. The discipline is too severe.

During the practice of pranayama there are certain perceptible stages. They are given in the text.

In the beginning there is perspiration, in the middle stage there is quivering, and in the last or the third stage one obtains steadiness; and then the breath should be made steady or motionless. The perspiration exuding from exertion of practice should be rubbed into the body (and not wiped) i.e. by so doing the body becomes strong and light.[26]

I experienced the first stage at the very onset. After one or two rounds the perspiration began to flow freely. As I developed strength and power, it was slower in making its appearance and was not so extreme as when I was straining. It was several weeks before I observed the second stage, quivering, and this was at a time when I was perfecting bhastrika. First there appeared itching sensations. As I continued the practice, the sensations increased. Soon I began to feel as though bugs

---

25) See *Siva Samhita*, iii, 53–4: "Then gradually he should make himself able to practise for three Ghatis (one hour and a half a time, he should be able to restrain breath for that period). Through this, the Yogi undoubtedly obtains all the longed-for powers. The Yogi acquires the following powers: Vakya Siddhi (prophecy), transporting himself everywhere at will (Kamachari), clairvoyance (duradrishti), clairaudience (durasrute), subtle-sight (Suksmadristi), and the power of entering another's body (Parakayapravesana), turning base metal into gold by rubbing them with his excrements and urine, and the power of becoming invisible, and lastly, moving in the air."

26) *Hatha Yoga Pradipika*, ii, 12–13. Compare Siva Samhita, iii, 40–I: "In the first stage of Pranayama, the body of the Yogi begins to perspire. When it perspires he should rub it well, otherwise the body of the Yogi loses in Dhatu (humours). In the second stage there takes place the trembling of the body; in the third, the jumping about like a frog; and when the practice becomes greater, the adept walks in the air."

were crawling over my body. While I was working, my leg would suddenly shake. Later, other muscles unexpectedly contracted, and soon my whole body would shake beyond control. At this time I was told always to use the padmasana posture. This prevented the body from going into convulsions. By adhering to my schedule, these manifestations all passed away. Another trying experience resulted from the agonizing pains that pierced the abdominal cavity. At first there were loud croaking noises as the intestines became filled with air. This was caused by swallowing the air as it tried to find its way out. The increased pressure was the source of this problem; but I was told that it would cease in time, and it did. At such periods, if one does not have an understanding of the principles upon which the practices are based, his faith is likely to forsake him. It is difficult to hold in mind the advice of the text: "Verily there are many hard and almost unsurmountable obstacles in Yoga, yet the Yogi should go on with his practice at all hazards; even were his life to come to the throat."[27]

The purpose of pranayama is to produce certain psychological phenomena; but this requires special techniques, which will be described in the next chapter. However, there are some specific physical results that are supposed to be observable. The text says:

When the body becomes lean, the face transparent, Anahatanada manifest, and the eyes are clear, the body is healthy, bindu [semen] under control, appetite increases, and the Nadis are purified, there are the signs of success in Hatha Yoga.[28]

I had always kept myself in fair physical condition; so it is difficult to report specific causes of these results; however, these bodily conditions made themselves evident in my case, though I cannot attach any one

of them to any one exercise.

---

27) *Siva Samhita*, iii, 47.

28) *Hatha Yoga Pradipika*, ii, 78. Compare Siva Samhita, iii, 43–6: "… from the perfection of Pranayama follow decrease of sleep, excrements and urine. The truth-perceiving Yogi becomes free from disease, and sorrow or afflictions; he never gets (putrid) perspiration, saliva and intestinal worms. When in the body of the practitioner, there is neither any increase of phlegm, wind, nor bile; then he may with impunity be irregular in his diet and the rest. No injurious results then would follow, were the Yogi to take a large quantity of food, or very little, or no food at all. Through the strength of constant practice, the Yogi obtains Bhuchari-siddhi [Moving on the earth], he moves as the frog jumps over the ground, when frightened away by the clapping of hands." I experienced many of these signs.

MUDRAS

SPECIAL techniques are required to awaken the 'spiritual force' which is latent within man according to the theory of Hatha Yoga.[1] This subtle force is called Kundalini[2] and is believed to be in a static state. The aim and goal of Hatha Yoga is to enliven, or 'awaken', this force. After the student has purified his system and gained control of his breath, these techniques, called 'mudras',[3] are given to him by the guru according to his needs.

The purpose and importance of mudras is revealed by the text in typical allegorical fashion.

As the chief of the snakes is the support of the earth with all the mountains and forests on it, so all the Tantras (Yoga practices) rest on the Kundalini. When the sleeping Kundalini awakens by favour of a Guru, then all the lotuses (in the six chakras or centres) and all the knots are pierced through. Susumna (Sunya Padavi) becomes a main road for the passage of Prana, and the mind then becomes free from all connections (with its objects of enjoyment) and Death is then evaded. Susumna, Sunya Padavi, Brahma-Randhra, Maha-Patha, Smasana, Sambhavi, Madhya-Marga, are names of one and the same thing. In order, therefore, to awaken this goddess, who is sleeping at the entrance of Brahma Dvara (the great door), Mudras should be practised. Maha Mudra, Maha Bandha, Maha Vedha, Khecari, Uddiyana Bandha, Mula Bandha, Jalandhara Bandha, Viparita Karani, Vajroli, and Sakti Calani. These are the ten Mudras which annihilate old age and death. They have been explained by Adi Natha (Siva) and give eight kinds of divine wealth. They are loved by all the Siddhas (perfected ones) and are hard to attain even by the Maruts. These Mudras should be kept secret by every means, as one keeps one's box of jewelry, and should on no account be told to anyone, just as husband and wife keep their dealings secret.[4]

---

1) See Serpent Power—the chapter on the "Theoretical Basis of Yoga".

2) *Ibid.*; the chapter on "Embodied Consciousness". See also the discussion of this force by Briggs, in his *Gorakhnath and the Kanphata Yogis*, pp. 308 ff.

3) The word 'mudra' means 'to seal, close, or lock up'. The various practices are techniques for locking the breath within the body. Another term that is used in connection with these practices is 'bandha', which means 'to bind, fix, or restrain'. The distinction is theoretical and should not cause any confusion, for they are one and the same thing.

4) *Hatha Yoga Pradipika*, iii, 1–9. Compare *Gheranda Samhita*, iii, 1–3: "There are twenty-five

Each mudra has a specific purpose. It is not necessary to use every one of them when practising; yet it is advisable that the student be familiar with them. I shall, therefore, present all the general description and comments given in our text, as well as my personal experience. The text begins with maha-mudra (see Plate VII).

Pressing the Yoni (perineum) with the heel of the left foot, and stretching forth the right foot, its toe should be firmly grasped by the hands. By stopping the throat (by Jalandhara) the air is held upwards. Just as a snake struck with a stick becomes straight like a stick, in the same way, Sakti (Susumna) becomes straight at once. Then the Kundalini becomes as it were dead, leaving the support of both the Ida and the Pingala (the left and right sympathetic nervous system). The air should be expelled then, slowly only and not violently. For this very reason the best of the wise men call it the Maha Mudra. This Maha Mudra has been propounded by great masters. Great evils and pains, like death, are destroyed by it, and for this reason wise men call it the Maha Mudra. Having practised with the left nostril, it should be practised with the right one; and when the number on both sides becomes equal, then the Mudra should be discontinued. There is no food wholesome or injurious in this practice; for the practice of this Mudra destroys the injurious effects of all the rasas (chemicals). Even the deadliest of poisons, if taken, acts like nectar. Consumption, leprosy, prolapsus ani, colic, and the diseases due to indigestion—all

mudras, the practice of which gives success to the Yogins. They are: (1) Maha-mudra, (2) Nabho-mudra, (3) Uddiyana, (4) Jalandhara, (5) Mulabandha, (6) Mahabandha, (7) Mahavedha, (8) Khecari, (9) Viparitakarani, (10) Yoni-mudra, (11) Vajroli-mudra, (12) Sakticalani, (13) Tadagi, (14) Manduki, (15) Sambhavi, (16) Pancadharana (five dharanas), (21) Asvini, (22) Pasini, (23) Kaki, (24) Matangi, and (25) Bhujangini."

Compare *Siva Samhita*, iv, 12–15: "Now I shall tell you the best means of attaining success in Yoga. The practitioners should keep it secret. It is the inaccessible Yoga. When the sleeping goddess Kundalini is awakened through the grace of Guru, then all the lotuses and the bonds are readily pierced through and through. Therefore, in order that the goddess, who is asleep in the mouth of the Brahmarandhra (the innermost hollow of Susumna), be awakened, the Mudras should be practised with the greatest care. Out of the many Mudras the following ten are the best:—(l) Maha-mudra. (2) Mahabandha, (3) Mahavedha, (4) Khecari, (5) Jalandhara, (6) Mulabandha, (7) Viparitaka-rana, (8) Uddana, (9) Vajroni, and (10) Sakticalana." I will comment in the proper sequence on the additional mudras mentioned in the *Gheranda Samhita*.

Compare *Gheranda Samhita*, iii, 94–100: "O Canda-Kapali! thus have I recited to thee the chapter on Mudras. This is beloved of all adepts, and destroys decay and death. This should not be taught indiscriminately, nor to a wicked person, nor to one devoid of faith; this secret should be preserved with great care; it is difficult to be attained even by the Devas. These Mudras which give happiness and emancipation should be taught to a guileless, calm and peace-minded person, who is devoted to his Teacher and comes of good family. These Mudras destroy all diseases. They increase the gastric fire of him who practises them daily. To him death never comes, nor decays, etc.; there is no fear to him from fire and water, nor from air. Cough, asthma, enlargement of the spleen, leprosy, phlegm diseases of twenty sorts, are verily destroyed by the practice of these Mudras. O Canda! What more shall I tell thee? In short, there is nothing in this world like the Mudras for giving quick success."

these irregularities are removed by the practice of this Maha Mudra. This Maha Mudra has been described as the giver of great success (Siddhi) to men. It should be kept secret by every effort and not revealed to any and every one.[5]

A few supplementary remarks which were given to me by my teacher will be helpful. The technique is simple. Sit on the floor with both legs straight ahead, then place the heel of the left foot on the perineum. The next step is to grasp the great toe of the right foot and lean forward until the forehead rests on the knee of the extended leg. It is permissible to lock both hands around the ball of the foot instead of trying to keep a grip on the great toe. In the beginning I was permitted to grasp the ankle. While in this position, inhale and suspend as in all breathing exercises. The texts instruct the student to take in the breath through the left nostril; however, I was permitted to use both nostrils. During the suspension other mudras should be used to lock in the air and create internal pressure. This is done by using the chin

---

5) *Hatha Yoga Pradıpıka*, iii, 10–18. Compare *Gheranda Samhita*, iii, 6–8: "Pressing carefully the anus by the left heel, stretch the right leg and take hold of the toes by the hands; contract the throat (not exhaling), and fix the gaze between the eyebrows. This is called Maha-mudra by the wise. The practice of Maha-mudra cures consumption, the obstruction of the bowels, the enlargement of the spleen, indigestion and fever—in fact it cures all diseases!" I was taught to alternate the legs while learning.

Compare *Siva Samhita*, iv, 16–20: "My dearest, I shall now describe to you the Mahamudra, from whose knowledge the ancient sages Kapila and others, obtained successes in Yoga. In accordance with the instructions of the Guru, press gently on the perineum with the heel of the left foot. Stretching the right foot out, hold it fast by the two hands. Having closed the nine gates (of the body), place the chin on the chest. Then concentrate the vibrations of the mind and inspire air and retain it by kumbhaka (so long as one can comfortably keep it). This is Mahamudra, held secret in all the Tantras. The steady-minded Yogi, having practised it on the left side, should then practise it on the right side; and in all cases must be firm in Pranayama, —the regulation of his breath. In this way, even the most unfortunate Yogi might obtain success. By this means all the vessels of the body are roused and stirred into activity; the life is increased and its decay is checked, and all sins are destroyed. All diseases are healed and the gastric fire is increased. It gives faultless beauty to the body, and destroys decay and death. All fruits of desires and pleasures are obtained, and the senses are conquered. The Yogi fixed in meditation acquires all the above-mentioned things, through practice. There should be no hesitation in doing so. O ye worshipped of god! Know that this Mudra is to be kept secret with the greatest care. Obtaining this, the Yogi crosses the ocean of the world. This Mudra, described by me, is the giver of all desires to the practitioner; it should be practised in secrecy, and ought never to be given to everybody."

lock,[6] uddiyana,[7] and contraction of the anal sphincters.[8] Then the eyes should be closed and the mind focused on the space between the eyebrows. In this position the various inner lights are said to appear, which I shall discuss after I have described the physical techniques. After a suspension with the right leg extended, I was taught to reverse the legs and perform an equal number of suspensions with the left leg extended.

The next practice is maha bandha (the great binding).

Press the left heel to the perineum and place the right foot on the left thigh. Fill in the air, keeping the chin firm against the chest, and, having pressed the air, the mind should be fixed on the middle of the eyebrows or in the susumna (the spine). Having kept it confined so long as possible, it should be expelled slowly. Having practised on the left side, it should be practised again on the right side. Some are of opinion that the closing of the throat is not necessary here, and that keeping the tongue pressed against the roots of the two upper central teeth makes a good Bandha (stop). This stops the upward motion of all the Nadis. Verily this Maha Bandha is the giver of great Siddhis. This Maha Bandha is the most skilful means for cutting away the snare of death. It brings about the conjunction of the Triveni (Ida, Pingala and Susumna) and carries the mind to Kedara (the space between the eyebrows, which is the seat of Siva).[9]

In addition to what is given in the text, I was taught two sup-

6) See below, p. 76-77.

7) See above, pp. 42–43.

8) See below, p. 75–76.

9) *Hatha Yoga Pradipika*, iii, 19–24, Compare *Gheranda Samhita*, iii, 18–20: "Close the anal orifice by the heel of the left foot, press that heel with the right foot carefully, move slowly the muscles of the rectum, and slowly contract the muscles of the yoni or perineum (space between the anus and the Scrotum): restrain the breath by Jalandhara. This is called Mahabandha. The Mahabandha is the Greatest Bandha; it destroys decay and death: by virtue of this Bandha a man accomplishes all his desires."

Compare *Siva Samhita*, iv, 21–2: "Then (after Mahamudra), having extended the (right) foot, place it on the (left) thigh; contract the perineum, and draw the Apana Vayu upwards and join it with the Samana Vayu; bend the Prana Vayu downwards, and then let the wise Yogi bind them in trinity in the navel (i.e. the Prana and the Apana should be joined with Samana in the navel). I have told you now the Mahabandha, which shows the way to emancipation. By this, all the fluids in the vessels of the body of the Yogi are propelled towards the head. This should be practised with great care, alternately with both feet. Through this practice, the wind enters the middle channel of the Susumna, the body is invigorated by it, the bones are firmly knitted, the heart of the Yogi becomes full (of cheerfulness). By this Bandha, the great Yogi accomplishes all his desires."

plementary requirements. During the suspension I was told to draw in the abdominal viscera toward the spine, as in uddiyana, and then to work the muscles of the rectum forcibly. The contractions of the anal sphincters were to be continued until it was possible finally to draw in air, which was to be carried to the small intestines. I found no particular difficulty in doing this; however, it will be virtually impossible for anyone who has not perfected the practices required in the earlier stages. Here I was taught to use the alternate breath and to practise on both sides as in maha mudra.

The importance of the next practice can be seen from the way it is introduced by the text.

As beauty and loveliness do not avail a woman without a husband, so the Maha Mudra and the Maha Bandha are useless without the Maha Vedha [The Great Piercing]. Sitting with the Maha Bandha, the Yogi should fill in the air and keep his mind collected. The movements of the Vayus (Prana and Apana) should be stopped by closing the throat. Resting both the hands equally on the ground, he should raise himself a little and strike his buttocks against the ground gently. The air, leaving both the passages (Ida and Pingala), starts into the middle one. The union of the Ida and the Pingala and Agni is effected, in order to bring about immortality. When the air becomes as it were dead (by leaving its course through the Ida and Pingala) (i.e. when it has been kept confined), then it should be expelled. The practice of this Maha Vedha, the giver of great Siddhi, destroys old age, grey hair, and shaking of the body, and, therefore, it is practised by the best masters. These three are the great secrets. They are the destroyers of old age and death, increase the appetite, confer the accomplishments of Anima, etc. They should be practised eight times every day, once every three hours. They increase collection of good actions and lessen the evil ones. People, instructed well, should begin their practice, little by little, first.[10]

---

10) *Hatha Yoga Pradipika*, iii, 25–31. Compare *Gheranda Samhita*, iii, 21-4: "As the beauty and charms of women are in vain without men, so are Mulabandha and Mahabandha without Mahavedha. Sit first in Mahabandha posture, then restrain breath by Uddana Kumbhaka. This is called Mahavedha-the giver of success to the Yogis. The Yogin who daily practises Mahabandha and Mulabandha, accompanied with Mahavedha, is the best of Yogins. For him there is no fear of death, and decay does not approach. This Vedha should be kept carefully secret by the Yogins."

Compare Siva Samhita, iv, 23–30: "O goddess of the three worlds! when the Yogi, while performing the Mahabandha, causes the union of the Prana and Apana Vayus and filling in the viscera with air drives it slowly towards the nates, it is called Mahavedha. The best of the Yogis having, through the help of the Vayu, pierced with this perforator the knot which is in the path of Susumna, should then pierce the knot of Brahma. He who practises this Mahavedha with great secrecy, obtains Vayu-siddhi (success over the wind). It destroys decay and death. The gods residing in the chakras tremble owing to the gentle influx and efflux of air in Pranayama; the great goddess, Kundali Maha Maya, is also absorbed in the mount Kailasa. The Mahamudra and Mahabandha become

I was taught that instead of sitting in the posture described for maha-bandha, I was to use padmasana, then inhale, suspend, and do the chin-lock. While holding my breath I was to contract the anus and navel as though trying to bring them together. Next I was to lift my body from the floor and gently drop it in order to give it a slight jar. I was cautioned never to be severe when the air was locked within, for there is always danger of driving it into channels where it might prove harmful. This warning I heeded, and I cannot report any ill consequences. When the breath can no longer be held, relax the contraction of the anal sphincters and the abdominal muscles, but maintain the chin lock, while letting the air out very slowly. The effectiveness of these mudras cannot be seen until one has developed his pranayama, and even then it is necessary to practise them for some time before their purpose can be experienced. However, it is maintained by some teachers that a few of them can be used for building up the health of the body. I have always practised them in conjunction with pranayama and cannot report on their individual advantages. They are intended to produce certain mental conditions, which will be discussed later.

The fourth mudra listed in the text is described at length.

The Khecari Mudra [roaming through space, flying—a supernatural power of Yogis] is accomplished by thrusting the tongue into the gullet, by turning it over itself and keeping the eyesight in the middle of the eyebrows. To accomplish this, the tongue is lengthened by cutting the fraenum linguae, moving, and pulling it. When it can touch the space between the eyebrows, then Khecari can be accomplished. Taking a sharp, smooth, and clean instrument, of the shape of a cactus leaf, the fraenum of the tongue should be cut a little (as much as a hair's thickness), at a time. Then rock salt and yellow myrobalan (both powdered) should be rubbed in. On the 7th day, it should again be cut a hair's breadth. One should go on doing thus, regularly for six months. At the end of six months the fraenum of the tongue will be completely cut. Turning the tongue upwards, it is fixed on the three ways (oesophagus, windpipe and palate). Thus it makes the Khecari Mudra, and is called the Vyoma [Sky] Chakra. The Yogi who sits for a minute turning his tongue upwards is saved from poisons, diseases, death, old age, etc. He who knows the Khecari Mudra is not afflicted with disease, death, sloth, sleep, hunger, thirst, and

fruitless if they are not followed by Mahavedha; therefore, the Yogi should practise all these three successively with great care. He who practises these three daily four times with great care, undoubtedly conquers death within six months. Only the, siddha knows the importance of these three and no one else; knowing these, the practitioner obtains all success. This should be kept in great secrecy by the practitioner desirous of obtaining power; otherwise it is certain that the coveted powers can never be obtained through the practice of Mudras."

swooning. He who knows Khecari Mudra is not troubled by diseases, is not stained with karmas, and is not snared by time.[11]

The text continues to offer praise to this mudra. I feel it advisable to quote these general remarks in order to enable the reader to familiarize himself with the obscure and mysterious manner in which the material is handled in the traditional literature and the problems involved in trying to ferret out the true meaning of these teachings.

The Siddhas have named this Mudra Khecari from the fact that the mind and the tongue reach Akasa [Ether] by its practice. If the hole behind the soft palate be stopped with Khecari by turning the tongue upwards, then bindu (semen) cannot leave its place even if a woman were embraced. If the Yogi drinks Somarasa [vital fluid] by sitting with the tongue turned backwards and mind concentrated, there is no doubt he conquers death within 15 days. If the Yogi, whose body is full of Somarasa [vital fluid] were bitten by Taksaka (snake), its poison cannot permeate his body. As fire is inseparably connected with the wood and light is connected with the wick and oil, so does the soul not leave the body full of nectar exuding from the Soma ['Lunar' centre of vital fluid, located in the head]. Those who eat the flesh of the cow and drink the immortal liquor daily, are regarded by me men of noble family. Others are but a disgrace to their families. The word *go* (cow) means tongue; eating it is thrusting it in the gullet, which destroys great sins. Immortal liquor is the nectar exuding from the moon (Chandra situated on the left side of the space between the eyebrows). It is produced by the fire which is generated by thrusting the tongue. If the tongue can touch with its end the hole from which falls the rasa [vital fluid] which is saltish, bitter, sour, milky and similar to ghee and honey, one can drive away disease, can destroy old age, can evade an attack of arms, can become thrice immortal and can attract fairies. He who drinks the

---

11) *Hatha Yoga Pradipika*, iii, 32–40. Compare *Gheranda Samhita*, iii, 25-8: "Cut the lower tendon of the tongue, and move the tongue constantly; rub it with fresh butter, and draw it out (to lengthen it) with an iron instrument. By practising this always, the tongue becomes long, and when it reaches the space between the eyebrows, then the Khecari is accomplished. Then (the tongue being lengthened) practise turning it upwards and backwards so as to touch the palate, till at length it reaches the holes of the nostrils opening into the mouth. Close those holes with the tongue (thus stopping inspiration), and fix the gaze on the space between the eyebrows. This is called Khecari. By this practice there is neither fainting, nor hunger, nor thirst, nor laziness. There comes neither disease, nor decay, nor death. The body becomes divine."

Compare Siva Samhita, iv, 31–2: "The wise Yogi, sitting in Vajrasana posture, in a place free from all disturbance, should firmly fix his gaze on the spot in the middle of the two eyebrows; and reversing the tongue backwards fix it in the hollow under the epiglottis, placing it with great care on the mouth of the well of nectar (i.e. closing up the air passage). This mudra, described by me at the request of my devotees, is the Khecari Mudra. O, my beloved! Know this to be the source of all success, always practising it let him drink the ambrosia daily. By this he obtains Vigraha-siddhi (power over the microcosm), even as lion over the elephant of death."

clear stream of liquor of the moon (soma) falling from the brain to the sixteen petalled lotus (in the heart), obtained by means of Prana, by applying the tongue to the hole of the pendant in the palate, and by meditating on the great power (Kundalini), becomes free from disease and tender in body, like the stalk of a lotus, and the Yogi lives a very long life. On top of the Meru (spinal column), concealed in a hole, is the Somarasa (nectar of Chandra), the wise, whose intellect is not overpowered by Raja and Tama gunas, but in whom Sattva guna is predominant, say there is the (universal spirit) atma in it. It is the source of the down-going Ida, Pingala and Susumna Nadis, which are the Ganga, the Yamuna and the Sarasvati. From that Chandra is shed the essence which, leaving the body, causes death in men. It should, therefore, be stopped from shedding.[12] This (Khecari Mudra) is a very good instrument for this purpose. There is no other means of achieving this end. This hole is the generator of knowledge and is the source of the five streams (Ida, Pingala, etc.). In that colourless vacuum, Khecari Mudra should be established. There is only one seed germinating the whole universe from it; and there is only one Mudra, called Khecari. There is only one deva (god) without any one's support, and there is one condition called Manonmani.[13]

Aside from all the allegorical praise offered in reverence to khecari mudra, it is a very important technique for the practice of the more highly developed stages of Yoga and should be learned. This mudra is obviously important in connection with the control of the breath (see above, p. 61) but, as the passages just quoted indicate, it is central to much in the Yoga discipline because of the conflux of powers in the

---

12) I shall not pause to explain the elaborate mythology contained in this passage or indicate the physiological processes which they symbolize. This has been done by other writers. See Briggs, *Gorakhnath and the Kanphata Yogis*, ch. xv, and Rele, *The Mysterious Kundalini, passim*.

13) *Hatha Yoga Pradipika*, iii, 41–53. Compare *Gheranda Samhita*, iii, 29–32: "The body cannot be burned by fire, nor dried up by air, nor wetted by water, nor bitten by snakes. The body becomes beautiful; Samadhi is verily attained, and the tongue touching the holes in the roof (of the mouth) obtains various juices (it drinks nectar). Various juices being produced, day by day the man experiences new sensations; first, he experiences a saltish taste, then alkaline, then bitter, then astringent, then he feels the taste of butter, then of ghee, then of milk, then of curds, then of whey, then of honey, then of palm juice, and, lastly, arises the taste of nectar."
Compare *Siva Samhita*, iv, 33–7 "Whether pure or impure, in whatever condition one may be, if success be obtained in Khecari, he becomes pure. There is no doubt of it. He who practises it even for a moment crosses the great ocean of sins, and having enjoyed the pleasures of Deva-world is born into a noble family. He who practises this Khecari-Mudra calmly and without laziness counts as seconds the periods of a hundred Brahmas. He knows this Khecari-Mudra according to the instructions of his Guru, obtains the highest end, though immersed in great sins. O, ye adored of gods! This Mudra, dear as life, should not be given to everybody; it should be kept concealed with great care." In order to understand what is meant by these references on conquering death and enjoying the pleasures of Deva-world, see The Tibetan Book of the Dead, by W. Y. Evans-Wentz, which contains a discussion of this subject.

chakra of the head. Its chief purpose, as mythologically indicated here, is to keep the vital fluid in the head from dripping down (shedding) into the lower chakras.

The process itself is simple enough. I started by milking the tongue. This was accomplished by washing it and then catching hold of it with a linen towel. Any sort of cloth can be used, but I found this to be the most convenient. When the tongue has become sufficiently dry, it can be handled with the bare hands; but the slightest bit of saliva makes it impossible to handle it without the aid of a piece of cloth. I pulled it straight out and then from side to side as far as it would go. This I did regularly twice a day for ten minutes. After a couple of weeks I noticed that the fraenum was beginning to give way because of being drawn over the incisor teeth; but I wanted to encourage the process, so I resorted to a razor blade. Each morning I delicately drew the blade across the fraenum until blood appeared. There was no pain, and the bleeding stopped before I finished milking the tongue. The following morning the wound had begun to heal and a light tissue was beginning to form, which I scraped off; then I repeated the process of the preceding day.

I was also taught a practice supplementary to milking the tongue. In order to get the tongue down the throat, it is first necessary to loosen the soft palate. The most convenient way is to bend the end of the handle of an ordinary teaspoon enough to form a hook. Insert this in the back of the throat and draw it forward until it catches on to the palate ridge. When a firm grip has been secured, repeatedly pull the palate toward the front part of the mouth. In time this membrane will become so flexible that it will be almost possible to touch the teeth with the soft palate. I practised this daily for ten minutes after milking the tongue.

Success depends upon the amount of time spent in practice. I was able to accomplish it in about four months by working an average of ten minutes a day. For part of this period I worked ten minutes twice a day on each practice, and then circumstances made it necessary to set the practice aside for a few days a week. Sometimes I was able to devote only five minutes to each practice in the morning, having to forgo the evening round. To elongate the tongue so that it can be placed between the eyebrows requires several years, but it is not necessary to achieve this goal at once. It is sufficient to acquire the ability to swallow the tongue and to use it to direct the breath into the desired nostril or shut it off completely. During the practice of pranayama, it is the common practice to lock in the air by swallowing the tongue, but those who are unable to do this may turn the tongue upward and hold it firmly against the roof of the mouth.[14]

In the beginning I was permitted to help the tongue down the throat with the fingers, but after a time this was not necessary. As soon as I placed the tongue behind the palate, the saliva began to flow in a constant stream. In this way I was supposed to determine the condition of the body fluids. At first it was thick, heavy, and slimy; eventually, it became thin, clear, and smooth. Under my working conditions it was impractical—even impossible—for me to do more than make note of changes that I could see and feel. As the saliva accumulated in my mouth, I had to withdraw my tongue from behind my palate in order to swallow. Later I learned to swallow while holding my tongue in position, and finally I developed the practice so that I could leave it so placed for hours at a time, withdrawing it only when it was necessary to speak, eat, or engage in some other activity that made its position inconvenient.

As for the effectiveness of the practice, I can report that I did notice a lack of hunger and thirst when using it. One of the problems that confront the student when practising Yoga is how to satisfy the feeling of hunger without crowding the system with food. By using this practice I was able to subdue the hunger pangs so that it was necessary to eat only at the appointed time, without any of the reactions that would otherwise have ensued from the sparse diet. This mudra is also needed for the practice of pranayama. After holding the breath for several minutes a natural reflex makes one start to breathe again. I was told to use this practice, and I found that it helped to overcome that powerful urge. According to the teachings of Yoga the nerve

14)   See *Gheranda Samhita*, iii, 9: "In whatever business a Yogin may be engaged, wherever he may be, let him always keep his tongue turned upwards (towards the soft palate), and restrain the breath. This is called Nabho-Mudra; it destroys the disease of the Yogins." 'Nabho' means 'sky, cloud, vapour' and has reference to the mystic nectar that is believed to be in the top of the head. This practice, as well as others, is intended to stimulate the flow of this nectar. See *ibid.*, 62: "Closing the mouth, move the tongue towards the palate, and taste slowly the nectar (flowing from the Thousand-petalled Lotus) [nerve centre situated at the crown of the head]. This is Manduki Mudra (Frog-mudra)." I was also taught to seal the tongue against the roof of the mouth without turning it back. This is sufficient for the beginner, but later Khecari will be needed.

that controls the reflex action is associated with the tongue and by so controlling the tongue it is possible to affect this nerve. Whether this be true or not, from the practical standpoint I found that the exercise enabled me to overcome the urge to breathe. I was required to learn khecari along with the purification practices, instead of waiting until the need for it arose during the later stages of my training. On account of the time involved in mastering this technique, I recommend the same sequence for others.

The practice of uddiyana was described earlier.[15] The next is mula bandha (the basic binding).

Pressing Yoni (Perineum) with the heel, contract up the anus. By drawing the Apana thus, Mula Bandha is made. The Apana, naturally inclining downward, is made to go up by force. This Mula Bandha is spoken of by Yogis as done by contracting the anus. Pressing the heel well against the anus, draw up the air by force, again and again till it (air) goes up. Prana and Apana, Nada and Bindu, uniting into one this way, gives success in Yoga undoubtedly. By the unification of Prana, and Apana, urine and excrements decrease. Even an old man becomes young by constantly practising this Mula Bandha. Going up the Apana enters the zone of fire, i.e. the stomach. The flame of fire struck by air is thereby lengthened. These, fire and Apana go to the naturally hot Prana, which then highly flares up the bodily fire. The Kundalini, which has been sleeping all this time, is heated by this fire and awakens well. It hisses and becomes straight like a serpent struck with a stick. It enters the Brahma Nadi just as a serpent enters its hole. Therefore, the Yogi should always practise this Mula Bandha.[16]

This mudra is one of the principal restraints in the practice of

---

15) See above, pp. 42, 43.

16) *Hatha Yoga Pradipika*, iii, 60-8. *Compare Gheranda Samhita*, iii, 14–17: "Press with the heel of the left foot the region between the anus and the scrotum, and contract the rectum; carefully press the intestines near the navel on the spine; and put the right heel on the organ of generation or pubes. This is called Mulabandha, destroyer of decay. The person who desires to cross the ocean of Samsara, let him go to a retired place, and practise in secrecy this mudra. By the practice of it, the Vayu (Prana) is controlled undoubtedly; let one silently practise this, without laziness, and with care."

Compare *Siva Samhita*, iv, 41–4: "Pressing well the anus with the heel, forcibly draw upwards the Apana Vayu slowly by practice. This is described as the Mulabandha—the destroyer of decay and death. If, in the course of the practice of this Mudra, the Yogi can unite the Apana with the Prana Vayu, then it becomes of course the Yoni-Mudra. He who has accomplished Yoni-Mudra, what can not be accomplished in this world. Sitting in the Padmasana posture, free from idleness, the Yogi leaving the ground, moves through the air, by virtue of this Mudra. If the wise Yogi is desirous of crossing the ocean of the world, let him practise this Bandha in secret, in a retired place."

pranayama. According to my instructions the important feature is the contraction of the anal sphincter while the abdominal viscera are held in as far as possible. I was taught to use the practice in any posture when I wanted to lock the air within and create internal pressure. I did not have to assume the siddhasana posture, with the heel pressing the perineum. From this it can be seen that whenever the text advises mula bandha, it means that one is to draw in the abdomen and contract the anus. In order to do this with sufficient force to effect results, one is required to practise uddiyana bandha and asvini mudra which, respectively, develop the muscles of the abdomen and the anus. I perfected these practices during the preliminary stages; so this technique caused me no trouble.

The practice of asvini[17] is not listed as a separate mudra, but it is an important technique and is required by all teachers. Some practices, such as basti, cannot be done until it is mastered. The object is to strengthen the rectal muscles so that it is possible to open the rectum at will. I was taught to take a position on elbows and knees. Exhale and pull the navel as far back toward the spine as possible; then contract the anal muscles, trying to pull the navel and the anus together. After a vigorous contraction, relax and breathe again. By the repeated practice of this contraction and relaxation complete control over the rectal muscles can be established. I was told that a normal person can accomplish this in about two weeks by practising an hour a day. The exercise was not assigned to me until I had perfected uddiyana and nauli, consequently I was able to perform it after a few attempts. In the end I found no difficulty in holding the rectum open without the suspension of breath.

Jalandhara bandha (cloud-holding, receptacle of vital fluid) is described as follows.

Contract the throat and press the chin firmly against the chest. This is called Jalandhara Bandha, which destroys old age and death. It stops the opening (hole) of the group of the Nadis, through which the juice from the sky (from the Soma or Chandra in the brain) falls down. It is, therefore, called the Jalandhara Bandha—the destroyer of a host of diseases of the throat. In Jalandhara Bandha,

---

17) See *Gheranda Samhita*, iii, 82–3: "Contract and dilate the anal aperture again and again; this is called Asvini-mudra. It awakens the Sakti (Kundalini). This Asvini is a great mudra; it destroys all diseases of the rectum; it gives strength and vigour, and prevents premature death."

by a perfect contraction of the throat, the nectar does not fall into the fire (the Surya situated in the navel), and the air is not disturbed. The two Nadis should be stopped firmly by contracting the throat. This is called the middle circuit or centre (Madhya Chakra) and it stops the 16 adharas (i.e. vital parts)[18] By drawing up the mulasthana (anus), Uddiyana Bandha should be performed. The flow of the air should be directed to the Susumna, by closing the Ida and the Pingala. The Prana becomes calm and latent by this means, and thus there is no death, old age disease, etc. These three Bandhas [19] are the best of all and have been practised by the masters. Of all the means of success in the Hatha Yoga, they are known to the Yogis as the chief ones. The whole of the nectar, which exudes from the Soma (Chandra) possessing divine qualities, is devoured by the Surya; and, owing to this the body becomes old. To remedy this, the opening of the Surya is avoided by excellent means. It is to be learnt best by instructions from a guru; but not by even a million discussions.[20]

The importance of jalandhara cannot be over-emphasized. It is popularly known as the chin lock and is required whenever one needs to seal the breath within the body during suspension. When I complained of tingling and buzzing sounds in my head toward the end of a suspension, I was advised to pay closer attention to this practice. By securely locking the chin into the jugular notch I was able to prevent these sounds and thereby to continue my breath suspension without this disagreeable experience, caused by the air in trying to find its way out. My only comment in addition to what the text has said about jalandhara is that I was taught always to simulate the act of swallowing

---

18) *Hatha Yoga Pradipika*, iii, 72, note: "The sixteen vital parts mentioned by renowned Yogis are the (1) thumb, (2) ankles, (3) knees, (4) thighs, (5) the prepuce, (6) organ of generation, (7) the navel, (8) the heart, (9) the neck, (10) the throat, (11) the palate, (12) the nose, (13) the middle of the eyebrows, (14) the forehead, (15) the head and (16) the Brahma randhra."

19) The three bandhas are: mula bandha, uddiyana bandha, and jalandhara.

20) *Hatha Yoga Pradipika*, iii, 69–77. Compare *Gheranda Samhita*, iii, 12–13: "Contracting the throat, place the chin on the chest. This is called Jalandhara. By this Bandha the sixteen Adharas are closed. This Maha-mudra destroys death. This success-giving Jalandhara when practised well for six months, the man becomes an adept without doubt."
Compare *Siva* Samhita, iv, 38-40 "Having contracted the muscles of the throat press the chin on the breast. This is said to be the Jalandhara-Mudra. Even gods reckon it as inestimable. The fire in the region of the navel (i.e. the gastric juice) drinks the nectar which exudes out of the thousand-petalled lotus. (In order to prevent the nectar to be thus consumed), he should practise this Bandha. Through this Bandha the wise Yogi himself drinks the nectar and, obtaining immortality, enjoys the three worlds. This Jalandhara-Bandha is the giver of success to the practitioner; the Yogi desirous of success should practise it daily."

a couple of times before using it.

The practice of viparita karani (inverted body) commonly known as the 'head-stand', has been described with the postures.[21] The next three mudras listed are vajroli, sahajoli (innate), and amaroli (immortal).[22]They are auxiliary techniques and did not form an integral part of my basic training, for success in the practice of Yoga is possible without them. Their purpose is to enable one to control the sex force of the body, which the Yogis recognize as a fundamental urge in human nature.

The object of Hatha Yoga is to vitalize the latent forces within man called Kundalini. The various mudras have been designed toward that ultimate end. The last practice given in the text, called sakti calani, assumes that all the previous steps have been perfected and that the student is ready to stir this dormant energy and thereby experience 'true reality'. I include the full statement of the text in order to show the stress laid on this aspect of the practices.

Kutilangi (crooked-bodied), Kundalini, Bhujangi (a she-serpent) Sakti, Isvari, Kundali, Arundhati, all these words are synonymous. As a door is opened with a key, so the Yogi opens the door of mukti by opening Kundalini by means

---

21) See above, p. 29

22) For the classical description see *Hatha Yoga Pradipika*, iii, 82–96: "Even one who lives a wayward life, without observing any rules of Yoga, but performs Vajroli, deserves success and is a Yogi. Two things are necessary for this, and these are difficult to get for the ordinary people—(1) milk and (2) a woman behaving, as desired. By practising to draw in the Bindu (semen), discharged during cohabitation, whether one be a man or a woman, one obtains success in the practice of Vajroli. By means of a pipe, one should blow air slowly into the passage in the male organ. By practice, the discharged Bindu is drawn up. One can draw back and preserve ones own discharged Bindu. The Yogi who can protect his Bindu thus, overcomes death; because death comes by discharging Bindu, and life is prolonged by its preservation. By preserving Bindu, the body of the Yogi emits a pleasing smell. There is no fear of death, so long as the Bindu is well established in the body. The Bindu of men is under the control of the mind, and life is dependent on the Bindu. Hence, mind and Bindu should be protected by all means.

"Sahajoli and amaroli are only the different kinds of Vajroli. Ashes from burnt up cow dung should be mixed with water. Being free from exercise of Vajroli, man and woman seated at ease, should both rub it on their bodies. This is called Sahajoli, and should be relied on by Yogis. It does good and gives moksa. This Yoga is achieved by courageous wise men, who are free from envy, and cannot be accomplished by the envious. In the doctrine of the sect of the Kapalikas, the Amaroli is the drinking of the cool mid stream; leaving the first, as it is a mixture of too much bile and the last which is useless. He who drinks Amari, snuffs it daily, and practises Vajroli, is called practising Amaroli. The Bindu discharged in the practice of Vajroli should be mixed with ashes, and the rubbing it on the head gives divine sight." The description of vajroli given in *Gheranda Samhita* is entirely different. For comparison see p. 29 n. *Siva Samhita* does not give it.

of Hatha Yoga. The Paramesvari (Kundalini) sleeps, covering with her mouth the hole of the passage by which one can go to the seat of Brahman which is free from pains. Kundali Sakti sleeps on the bulb, for the purpose of giving moksa to Yogis and bondage to the ignorant. He who knows it, knows Yoga. Kundali is of a coiled shape, and has been described to be like a serpent. He who has moved that Sakti is no doubt Mukta (released from bondage).

Yongster Tapasvini (a she-ascetic), lying between the Ganga and the Yamuna (Ida and Pingala) should be caught hold of by force, to get the highest position. Ida is called goddess Ganga, Pingala goddess Yamuna. In the middle of the Ida and the Pingala is the young widow Kundali. This sleeping she-serpent should be awakened by catching hold of her tail. By the force of Hatha the Sakti leaves her sleep and starts upwards. This she-serpent is situated in Muladhara. She should be caught and moved daily, morning and evening, for half a prahara (1½ hours), by filling with air through Pingala by the Paridhana method. The bulb is above the anus, a vitasti (twelve angulas) long, and measures four angulas (3 inches) in extent and is soft and white, and appears as if a folded cloth. Keeping the feet in Vajra-asana (Padma-asana) hold them firmly with the hands. The position of the bulb will then be near the ankle joint, where it should be pressed.

The Yogi, sitting with Vajra-asana and having moved Kundali, should perform Bhastrika to awaken Kundali soon. Bhanu (Surya, near the navel) should be contracted (by contracting the navel), which will move the Kundali. There is no fear for him who does so, even if he has entered the mouth of death. By moving this for two muhurtas, it is drawn up a little by entering the Susumna (spinal column). By this Kundalini leaves the entrance of the Susumna at once, and the Prana enters it of itself. Therefore, this comfortably sleeping Arundhati should always be moved; for by so doing the Yogi gets rid of diseases.

The Yogi observing Brachmacharya (continence) and always eating sparingly, gets success within forty days by practice with the Kundalini. After moving the Kundali, plenty of Bhastra should be performed. By such practice, he has no fear from the god of death. There is no other way, but the practice of the Kundali, for washing away the impurities of the 72,000 Nadis. This middle Nadi becomes straight by steady practice of postures, Pranayama and Mudras of Yogis. Those whose sleep has decreased by practice and mind has become calm by samadhi, get beneficial accomplishments by Sambhavi and other Mudras. Without Raja Yoga, this earth, the night, and the Mudras, be they howsoever wonderful, do not appear beautiful. All the practices relating to the air should be performed with concentrated mind. A wise man should not allow his mind to wander away. These are the ten Mudras, as explained by Adinatha (Siva). Every one of them is the giver of great accomplishments to the practiser. He is really the Guru and to be considered as Isvara in human form who teaches the Mudras as handed down from guru to guru. Engaging in practice, by putting faith in his words, one gets the Siddhis of Anima, etc.,[23] as also evades death.[24]

This awakening of Kundalini assumes that the student has thoroughly purified his nervous system according to the standards of Yoga and has perfected all the preliminary techniques. I was told that the best posture is the full padmasana, in which the hands are crossed behind the back and grasp the great toe of their respective feet. However, it is permissible to use siddhasana. After the posture has been assumed, start the practice of pranayama and use the three principal

---

23) Siddhi means "accomplishment, performance, fulfilment, (complete attainment, success." Here it has reference to the acquisition of the eight supernatural powers: (1) the power to assimilate oneself with an atom (anima); (2) the power to be as light as cotton or any similar thing (laghima); (3) the power of reaching anywhere, even to the moon (praptih); (4) the power of having all wishes of whatever description realized (prakamyam); (5) the power to expand oneself into space (mahima); (6) the power to create (isitvam); (7) the power to command all (vasitvam); (8) the power of suppressing desire (kamavasayita). Compare *Siva Samhita*, iii, 54; for description, see p. 61 *n*.

24) *Hatha Yoga Pradipika*, iii, 97–123. Compare *Gheranda Samhita*, iii, 49–60: "The great goddess Kundalini, the energy of Self, atma-sakti (spiritual force), sleeps in the Muladhara (rectum); she has the form of a serpent having three coils and a half. So long as she is asleep in the body, the Jiva is a mere animal, and true knowledge does not arise, though he may practise ten millions. As by a key a door is opened, so by awakening the Kundalini by Hatha Yoga, the door of Brahman is unlocked. Encircling the loins with a piece of cloth, seated in a secret room, not naked in an outer room, let him practise the Sakticalana. One cubit long, and four fingers (3 inches) wide, should be the encircling cloth, soft, white and of fine texture. Join this cloth with the Kati-Sutra (a string worn round the loins). Smear the body with ashes, sit in Siddhasana-posture, drawing the Prana-Vayu with the nostrils, forcibly join it with the Apana. Contract the rectum slowly by the Asvini Mudra, till the Vayu enters the Susumna, and manifests its presence. By restraining the breath by Kumbhaka in this way, the serpent Kundalini, feeling suffocated, awakes and rises upwards to the Brahmarandhra. Without the Sakticalana, the Yoni-Mudra is not complete or perfected; first the Calana should be practised, and then the Yoni-Mudra. O Canda-Kapali! Thus have I taught thee the Sakticalana. Preserve it with care and practise it daily. This mudra should be kept carefully concealed. It destroys decay and death. Therefore, the Yogin, desirous of perfection, should practise it. The Yogin who practises this daily acquires adeptship, attains Vigraha-siddhi and all his diseases are cured."
Compare *Siva Samhita*, iv, 53–8: "Let the wise Yogi forcibly and firmly draw up the goddess Kundali sleeping in the Adhara Lotus, by means of the Apana Vayu. This is Sakti-Calana Mudra, the giver of all powers. He who practises this Sakti-Calana Mudra, daily, gets increase of life and destruction of diseases. Leaving sleep, the serpent (i.e. the Kundalini) herself goes up; therefore, let the Yogi desirous of power practise this. He who practises always this best Sakti-Calana according to the instructions of his guru, obtains the Vigraha-siddhi which gives the powers of anima, etc., and has no fear of death. He who practises the Sakti-Calana for two seconds, and with care is very near to success. This Mudra should be practised by the Yogi in the proper posture. These are the ten Mudra whose equal there never was nor ever shall be; through the practice of any one of them, a person becomes a siddha and obtains success."

locks.[25] The suspension is supposed to suffocate the Serpent kundalini, making it awaken and rise up. In order to force kundalini into the central channel located within the spinal cord, I was told to practise bhastrika for a few minutes and then work 'Her' for one hour and thirty minutes by means of nauli. If I continued this routine for the period of one year, I was assured, I would achieve success. Any further delay was said to be due to impurities which still remained in the nadis. So far I have never had the time to test this technique. However, I did use the supplementary practices given to me for stimulating the nerve centre, where the latent force called Kundalini is said to be located. They are pasini mudra, vajroli mudra and yogasana.[26] In the next chapter I will relate the psychological effects which I experienced.

---

25) Mula bandha, uddiyana bandha, and jalandhara.

26) See p. 28 *n*.

SAMADHI

"NOW I will describe a regular method of attaining to Samadhi, which destroys death, is the means of obtaining happiness, and gives the Brahmananda (Brahmanbliss)."[1] All who adhere to the way of life prescribed by Yoga aspire to achieve this ultimate state of consciousness, which is referred to by many different names. "Raja Yoga, Samadhi, Unmani, Manonmani, Amaratva, Laya, Tattva, Sunya, Asunya, Parama Pada, Amanaska, Advaita, Nirabamba, Niranjana, Jivan Mukti, Sahaja, Turya, are all synonymous."[2] Various figures of speech are employed to suggest its content.

As salt being dissolved in water becomes one with it, so when Atma and mind become one, it is called Samadhi. When the Prana becomes lean (vigourless) and the mind becomes absorbed, then their becoming equal is called Samadhi. This equality of the self and the ultra self, when all Samkalpas [mental processes, ideation] cease to exist, is called Samadhi. Who can know the true greatness of the Raja Yoga? Knowledge, Mukti, Steadiness, and Siddhis can be learnt by instructions from a Guru alone. Indifference to worldly enjoyments is very difficult to obtain. It is very difficult to get the condition of Samadhi without the favour of a true Guru.[3]

The fruit appears after the static force called Kundalini is made dynamic.

By means of various postures and different Kumbhakas, when the great power (Kundali) awakens, then the Prana becomes absorbed in Sunya (Samadhi). The Yogi whose sakti has awakened, and who has renounced all actions, attains to the condition of Samadhi without any effort. When the Prana flows in the Susumna and the mind has entered sunya, then the Yogi is free from the effects of Karmas.[4]

The way to accomplish this end is told.

---

1) *Hatha Yoga Pradipika*, iv, 2.

2) *Ibid.*, 3–4.

3) *Ibid.*, 5–9.

4) *Ibid.*, 10–12.

Always living in a good locality and having known the secret of Susumna, which has a middle course, and making the Vayu move in it, (the Yogi) should restrain the Vayu in the Brahmarandhra [fontanel]. Time, in the form of night and day, is made by the sun and the moon. That the Susumna devours this time (death) even, is a great secret. In this body there are 72,000 openings of Nadis; of these, the Susumna, which has the Sambhavi Sakti [the Divine Energy (Sakti) of the 'Peaceful One' (Sambhu) i.e. Siva] in it, is the only important one, the rest are useless. By this Sakti Vayu enters the Susumna without restraint in him who has awakened the Kundali by the (gastric) fire. The Prana, flowing through the Susumna, brings about the condition of Manonmani (mindlessness); other practices are simply futile for the Yogi. By whom the breathing has been controlled, by him the activities of the mind also have been controlled; and conversely, by whom the activities of the mind have been controlled, by him the breathing also has been controlled.[5]

Mind is the master of the senses, and the breath is the master of the mind. The breath in its turn is subordinate to the laya (absorption), and that laya depends on the nada [sound]. This very laya is what is called moksa, or, being a sectarian, you may not call it moksa, but when the mind becomes absorbed, a sort of ecstasy is experienced. By the suspension of respiration and the annihilation of the enjoyments of the senses, when the mind becomes devoid of all the activities and remains changeless, then the Yogi attains to the Laya stage. When all the thoughts and activities arc destroyed, then the Laya stage is produced, to describe which is beyond the power of speech, being known by self-experience alone. They often speak of Laya, Laya; but what is meant by it? Laya is simply the forgetting of the objects of senses when the Vasanas (desires) [innate propensities] do not rise into existence again.[6]

The whole of this world and all the schemes of the mind are but the creations of thought. Discarding these thoughts and taking leave of all conjectures, O Rama! obtain peace. As camphor disappears in fire, and rock salt in water, so the mind united with the atma loses its identity. All that appears is the knowable, the mind is called knowledge. When the knowable and the knowledge, are both destroyed equally, then there is no second way (i.e., Duality is destroyed). All this movable and immovable world is the vision of the mind. When the mind has attained to the unmani avastha, there is no dvaita (from the absence of the working of the mind). Mind disappears by removing the knowable, and, on its disappearance, atma only remains behind.[7]

---

5) *Hatha Yoga Pradipika*, iv. 16–21.

6) *Ibid.,* 29–33.

7) *Ibid.,* 57–61.

Samadhi cannot be experienced until a condition of mindlessness has been created. All modifications of the thinking principle must cease; all thought forms must be removed, yet some form of awareness must remain. Without Yoga experience it is difficult to imagine what is meant; that is why teachers do not even try to explain. Therefore, I, too, pass by the theory of samadhi and describe the more practical aspects of Yoga.

The method used to absorb the mind and induce the mental condition called Samadhi,[8] described in the text, is commonly known as

---

8) There are several methods given in *Gheranda Samhita*, vii, 12–3: "The Samadhi is a great Yoga; it is acquired by great good fortune. It is obtained through the grace and kindness of the Guru, and by intense devotion to him. That Yogin quickly attains this beautiful practice of Samadhi, who has confidence (or faith) in knowledge, faith in his own Guru, faith in his own Self and whose mind (manas) awakens to intelligence from day to day. Separate the Manas from the body, and unite it with the Paramatman. This is known as Samadhi or Mukti, liberation from all states of consciousness. I am Brahman, I am nothing else, verily am I Brahman. I am not participator of sorrow, I am Existence, Intelligence, and Bliss; always free and one with Brahman. The Samadhi is four-fold, i.e. Dhyana, Nada, Rasananda, and Laya respectively accomplished by Sambhavi Mudra, Khecari Mudra, Bhramari Mudra, and Yoni-Mudra. The Bhakti-Yoga Samadhi is fifth, and Raja-Yoga Samadhi, attained through Mano-Murccha Kumbhaka, is the sixth form of Samadhi.

"DHYANA-YOGA SAMADHI: Performing the Sambhavi Mudra perceive the Atman. Having seen once the Brahman in a Bindu (point of light), fix the mind on that point. Bring the Atman in Kha (Ether), bring the Kha (Ether or Space) in the Atman. Thus seeing the Atman full of Kha (Space or Brahman), nothing will obstruct him. Being full of perpetual bliss, the man enters Samadhi (Trance or Ecstasy).

"NADA-YOGA SAMADHI: Turn the tongue upwards (closing the wind-passages), by performing the Khecari Mudra; by so doing, Samadhi (trance asphyxiation) will be induced; there is no necessity of performing anything else.

"RASANANDA-YOGA SAMADHI: Let him perform the Bhramari Kumbhaka, drawing in the air slowly: expel the air slowly and slowly, when a buzzing sound like that of a beetle arises. Let him carry the Manas and place it in the centre of this sound of beetle-humming. By so doing, there will be Samadhi and by this, knowledge of so'ham (I am He) arises, and a great happiness take places.

"LAYA-SIDDHI-YOGA SAMADHI: Performing the Yoni-Mudra let him imagine that he is Sakti, and with this feeling enjoy the bliss of Paramatman (and that both have been united in one). By this he becomes full of bliss, and realises Aham Brahman, 'I am Brahman.' This conduces to Advaita Samadhi.

"BHAKTI-YOGA SAMADHI: Let him contemplate within his heart his special Deity; let him be full of ecstasy by such contemplation; let him, with thrill, shed tears of happiness, and by so doing he will become entranced. This leads to Samadhi and Manonmani.

"RAJA-YOGA SAMADHI: Performing Manomurccha Kumbhaka, unite the Manas with the Atman. By this Union is obtained Raja-Yoga Samadhi.

"PRAISE OF SAMADHI: O Canda! thus have I told thee about Samadhi which leads to emancipation. Raja-Yoga Samadhi, Unmani, Sahajavastha are all synonyms, and mean the Union of Manas with Atman. Visnu is in water, Visnu is in the earth, Visnu is on the peak of the mountain; Visnu is in the midst of the volcanic fires and flames; the whole universe is full of Visnu. All those that walk on land or move in the air, all living and animate creation, trees, shrubs, roots, creepers and grass, etc., oceans and mountain—all, know ye to be Brahman. See them all in Atman. The Atman confined in

the 'practice of nada', or listening to the internal sound. It was highly recommended to me by various teachers in all parts of India. For the benefit of the reader I will include the full statement given in the text.

I will now describe the practice of anahata nada (heart sound), as propounded by Goraksa Natha for the benefit of those who are unable to understand the principles of knowledge—a method which is liked by the ignorant also. Adinatha propounded 1¼ crore [ten million] methods of trance and they are all extant. Of these, the hearing of the anahata nada (heart sound) is the only one, which is the chief, in my opinion. Sitting with Mukta Asana and with the Sambhavi Mudra, the Yogi should hear the sound inside his right ear, with collected mind. The ears, the eyes, the nose, and the mouth should be closed[9] and then the clear sound is heard in the

the body is Caitanya or Consciousness, it is without a second, the Eternal, the Highest; knowing it separate from body, let him be free from desires and passions. Thus is Samadhi obtained free from all desires. Free from attachment to his own body, to son, wife, friends, kinsmen, or riches; being free from all let him obtain fully the Samadhi. Siva has revealed many Tattvas, such as Laya Amrta, etc., of them, I have told thee an abstract, leading to emancipation. O Canda! thus have I told thee of Samadhi, difficult of attainment. By knowing this, there is no rebirth in this Sphere."

9) This is called 'yoni-mudra'. See *Gheranda Samhita,* iii, 37–44: 'Sitting in Siddhasana, close the ears with the thumbs, the eyes with the index fingers, the nostrils with the middle fingers, the upper lip with the ring-fingers, and the lower lip with the little fingers. Draw in the Prana-Vayu by Kakimudra and join it with the Apana-Vayu; contemplating the six chakras in their orders, let the wise one awaken the sleeping serpent-goddess Kundalini, by repeating the mantra Hum and Hamsa, and raising the Sakti (Force-kundalini) with the jiva, place her at the thousand-petalled lotus. Being himself full of Sakti, being joined with the great Siva, let him think of the Supreme Bliss. Let him contemplate on the union of Siva (spirit) and Sakti (force or energy) in this world. Being himself all bliss, let him realise that he is the Brahman. This Yoni mudra is a great secret, difficult to be obtained even by the Devas. By once obtaining perfection in its practice, one enters verily into Samadhi. By the practice of this Mudra, one is never polluted by the sins of killing a Brahmana, killing a foetus, drinking liquor, or polluting the bed of the Preceptor. All the mortal sins and the venal sins are completely destroyed by the practice of this Mudra. Let him therefore practise it, if he wishes for emancipation."

Compare *Siva Samhita*, iv, 1–11: "First with a strong inspiration fix the mind in the Adhara lotus (muladhara). Then engage in contracting the Yoni, which is situated in the perineal space. There let him contemplate that the God of Love resides in that Brahma Yoni and that he is beautiful like Bandhuk flower (Pentapetes Pheonicia—brilliant as tens of millions of suns, and cool as tens of millions of moons. Above this (Yoni) is a very small and subtle flame, whose form is intelligence. Then let him imagine that a union taker place there between himself and that flame (the Siva and Sakti). (Then imagine that)—There go up through the Susumna vessel, the three bodies in their due order (i.e. the etheric, the astral, and the mental bodies). There is emitted in every chakra the nectar, the characteristic of which is great bliss. Its colour is whitish rosy (pink), full of splendour, showering down in jets the immortal fluid. Let him drink this wine of immortality which is divine, and then again enter the Kula (i.e. perineal space). Then let him go again to the Kula through the practice of matra Yoga (i.e. pranayama). This Yoni has been called by me in the Tantras as equal to life. Again let him be absorbed in that Yoni, where dwells the fire of death—the nature of Siva etc.

passage of the Susumna which has been cleansed of all its impurities.[10]

The different stages of developments are determined according to the sounds which appear.

In all the Yogas, there are four states: (1) Arambha or the preliminary, (2) Ghata, or the state of a jar, (3) Parichaya (knowledge), (4) Nispatti (consummation).[11]

[The first stage]. Arambha Avastha, [is reached] when the Brahma granthi (in the heart) is pierced through by Pranayama, then a sort of happiness is experienced in the vacuum of the heart, and the anahata [the heart chakra] sounds, like various tinkling sounds of ornaments, are heard in the body. In the Arambha, a Yogi's body becomes divine, glowing, healthy, and emits a divine smell. The whole of his heart becomes void.[12]

Thus has been described by me the method of practising the great Yoni Mudra. From success in its practice, there is nothing which cannot be accomplished. Even those mantras which are deformed (chhinna) or paralysed (Kilita), scorched (stambhita) by fire, or whose flame has become attenuated, or which are dark, and ought to be abandoned, or which are evil, or too old, or which are proud of their budding youth, or have gone over to the side of the enemy, or weak and essenceless without vitality; or which have been divided into hundreds of parts, even they become fertile through time and method. All these can give powers and emancipation when properly given to the disciple by the Guru, after having initiated him according to proper rites, and bathed him a thousand times. This Yoni Mudra has been described, in order that the student may deserve (to be initiated into the mysteries of) and receive the mantras.

"He who practises Yoni Mudra is not polluted by sin were he to murder a thousand Brahmanas or kill all the inhabitants of the three worlds:—Were he to kill his teacher or drink wine or commit theft, or violate the bed of his preceptor, he is not stained by these sins also, by virtue of this mudra. Therefore, those who wish for emancipation should practise this daily. Through practice (abhyasa), success is obtained, through practice one gains liberation. Perfect conciousness is gained through practice. Yoga is attained through practice; success in Mudras comes by practice; through practice is gained success in pranayama. Death can be cheated of its prey through practice and man becomes the conqueror of death by practice. Through practice one gets the power of vah (prophecy), and the power of going everywhere, through mere exertion of will. This Yoni Mudra should be kept in great secrecy, and not be given to everybody. Even when threatened with death, it should not be revealed or given to others."

10)   *Hatha Yoga Pradipika*, iv. 64–7.

11)   *Hatha Yoga Pradipika*, iv, 68. Compare *Siva Samhita*, iii, 29: "In all kinds of Yoga, there are four stages of Pranayama:—1. Arambha-avastha (the state of beginning); 2. Ghata-avastha (the state of co-operation of Self and Higher Self); 3. Parichaya-avastha (knowledge); 4. Nishpatti-avastha (the final consummation).

12)   Hatha Yoga Pradipika, iv, 69–70. Compare *Siva Samhita*, iii, 27–9: "When thus the nadis of the truth perceiving Yogi are purified, then his defects being all destroyed, he enters the first stage in the practice of Yoga called Arambha. Certain signs are perceived in the body of the Yogi whose nadis have been purified. I shall describe, in brief, all these various signs. The body of the person practising the regulation of breath becomes harmoniously developed, emits sweet scent, and looks

In the second stage, [Ghata Avastha], the airs are united into one and begin moving in the middle channel. The Yogi's posture becomes firm, and he becomes wise like a god. By this means the Visnu knot (in the throat) is pierced which is indicated by the highest pleasure experienced, and then the Bheri sound (like the beating of a kettle drum) is evolved in the vacuum in the throat.[13]

In the third stage [Parichaya Avastha], the sound of a drum is known to arise in the Sunya between the eyebrows, and then the Vayu goes to the Mahasunya [Great Void], which is the home of all the siddhis. Conquering, then, the pleasures of the mind, ecstasy is spontaneously produced which is devoid of evils, pains, old age, disease, hunger and sleep.[14]

[The last stage, Nispatti Avastha, is reached] when the Rudra granthi is pierced and the air enters the seat of the Lord (the space between the eyebrows), then the perfect sound like that of a flute is produced. The union of the mind and the sound is called the Raja Yoga. The (real) Yogi becomes the creator and destroyer of the universe, like God. Perpetual happiness is achieved by this; I

---

beautiful and lovely…"

13) *Hatha Yoga Pradipika*, iv, 71–2. Compare *Siva Samhita*, iii, 55–9: "When by the practice of Pranayama, the Yogi reaches the state of Ghata (water-jar), then for him there is nothing in this circle of universe which he cannot accomplish. The Ghata is said to be that state in which the Prana and the Apana Vayus, the Nada and the Bindu, the Jivatma (the Human Spirit) and the Paramatma (the Universal Spirit) combine and co-operate. When he gets the power of holding breath (i.e. to be in trance) for three hours, then certainly the wonderful state of Pratyahara is reached without fail. Whatever object the Yogi perceives, let him consider it to be the spirit. When the modes of action of various senses are known, then they can be conquered. When, through great practice, the Yogi can perform one Kumbhaka for full three hours, when for eight Dandas (3 hours) the breathing of the Yogi is suspended, then that wise one can balance himself on his thumb; but he appears to others as insane."

14) *Hatha Yoga Pradipika*, iv, 73–4. Compare Siva Samhita, iii, 60–5: "After this, through exercise, the Yogi reaches the Parichaya Avastha. When the air leaving the sun and the moon (the right and the left nostrils), remains unmoved and steady in the ether of the tube Susumna, then it is in the Parichaya state. When he, by the practice of Yoga, acquires power of action (Kriya Sakti) and pierces through the six Chakras, and reaches the sure condition of Parichaya then the Yogi, verily, sees the three-fold effects of Karma. Then, let the Yogi destroy the multitude of Karmas by the Pranava (OM): let him accomplish Kayavyuha (a mystical process of arranging the various Skandhas [constituents] of the body), in order to enjoy or suffer the consequences of all his actions in one life without the necessity of rebirth. At that time let the great Yogi practise the five-fold Dharana forms of concentration on Visnu, by which command over the five elements is obtained, and fear of injuries from any one of them is removed (Earth, Water, Fire, Air, Ether cannot harm him). Let the wise Yogi practise Dharana thus:–five Ghatis (2½ hours) in the Adhara lotus (Muladhara); five Ghatis in the seat of the Linga (Svadhisthana), five Ghatis in the region above it, (in the navel, Manipura), and the same in the heart (Anahata); five Ghatis in the throat (Visuddha) and, lastly let him hold Dharana for five Ghatis in the space between the eyebrows (Ajnapur). By this practice the elements cease to cause any harm to the great Yogi. The wise Yogi, who thus continually practises concentration (Dharana), never dies through hundreds of cycles of the great Brahma."

do not care if the mukti be attained or not attained. This happiness, resulting from absorption (in Brahman), is obtained by means of Raja-Yoga. Those who are ignorant of the Raja-Yoga and practise only the Hatha Yoga, will in my opinion, waste their energy fruitlessly.[15]

Contemplation on the space between the eyebrows is, in my opinion, best for accomplishing soon the Unmani state. For people of small intellect, it is a very easy method for obtaining perfection in the Raja-Yoga. The Laya produced by nada (sound), at once gives experience (of spiritual powers). The happiness which increases in the hearts of Yogisvaras who have gained success in Samadhi by means of attention to the nada, is beyond description, and is known to Sri Guru Natha alone.

---

15) *Hatha Yoga Pradipika*, iv, 75–8. Compare *Siva Samhita*, iii, 66–83: "After this, through gradual exercise, the Yogi reaches the Nispatti Avastha (the condition of consummation). The Yogi, having destroyed all the seeds of Karma which existed from the beginning drinks the waters of immortality. When the Jivan-mukta (delivered in the present life), tranquil Yoga has obtained, through practice, the consummation of Samadhi (meditation), and when this state of consummated Samadhi can be voluntarily evoked, then let the Yogi take hold of the Chetana (conscious intelligence) together with the air, and with the force of (Kriyasakti) conquer the six wheels, and absorb it in the force called Jnana-sakti. Now we have described the management of the air in order to remove the troubles (which await the Yogi); through the knowledge of Vayusadhana vanish all sufferings and enjoyments in the circle of this universe. When the skilful Yogi, by placing the tongue at the root of the palate, can drink the Prana Vayu, then there occurs complete dissolution of all Yogas (i.e. he is no longer in need of Yoga). When the skilful Yogi, knowing the laws of the action of Prana and Apana, can drink the cold air through the contraction of the mouth, in the form of a crowbill, then he becomes entitled to liberation. That wise Yogi, who daily drinks the ambrosial air, according to proper rules, destroys fatigue, burning (fever), decay, and old age, and injuries. Pointing the tongue upwards, when the Yogi can drink the nectar flowing from the moon (situated between the two eyebrows) within a month he certainly would conquer death. When having firmly closed the glottis by the proper yogi method, and contemplating on the goddess Kundalini, he drinks (the moon fluid of immortality), he becomes a sage or poet within six months. When he drinks the air through the crow-bill, both in the morning and evening twilight, contemplating that it goes to the mouth of the Kundalini, consumption of the lungs (phthisis) is cured. When the wise Yogi drinks fluid day and night through the crow-beak, his diseases are destroyed; he acquires certainly the powers of clairaudience and clairvoyance. When firmly closing the teeth (by pressing the upper on the lower jaw), and placing the tongue upwards, the wise Yogi drinks the fluid very slowly, within a short period he conquers death. One, who daily continues this exercise for six months only, is freed from all sins, and destroys all diseases. If he continues this exercise for a year, he becomes a Bhairava; he obtains the powers of anima etc., and conquers all elements and the elementals. If the Yogi can remain for half a second with his tongue drawn upwards, he becomes free from disease, death, and old age. Verily, verily, I tell you the truth that the person never dies who contemplates by pressing the tongue, combined with the vital fluid or Prana. Through this exercise and Yoga, he becomes like a Kamadeva, without a rival. He feels neither hunger, nor thirst, nor sleep, nor swoon. Acting upon these methods the great Yogi becomes in the world perfectly independent; and freed from all obstacles, he can go everywhere. By practising thus, he is never reborn, nor is tainted by virtue and vice but enjoys (for ages) with the gods."

The sound which a muni [sage, ascetic] hears by closing his ears with his fingers, should be heard attentively, till the mind becomes steady in it. By practising with this nada, all other external sounds are stopped. The Yogi becomes happy by overcoming all distractions within fifteen days. In the beginning, the sounds heard are of a great variety and very loud; but as the practice increases, they become more and more subtle. In the first stage, the sounds are surging, thundering like the beating of kettle-drums, and jingling ones. In the intermediate stage, they are like those produced by conch, Mridanga, bells, etc. In the last stage, the sounds resemble those from tinklets, flute, Vina, bee, etc. These various kinds of sounds are heard as being produced in the body. Though hearing loud sounds like those of thunder, kettle-drums, etc., one should try to get in touch with subtle sounds only. Leaving the loudest, taking up the subtle one, and leaving the subtle one, taking up the loudest, thus practising, the distracted mind does not wander elsewhere.[16]

Wherever the mind attaches itself first, it becomes steady there; and then it becomes absorbed in it. Just as a bee, drinking sweet juice, does not care for the smell of the flower; so the mind, absorbed in the nada, does not desire the object of enjoyment. The mind, like an elephant, habituated to wander in the garden of enjoyments, is capable of being controlled by the sharp goad of anahata nada. The mind, captivated in the snare of nada, gives up all its activity; and, like a bird with clipped wings, becomes calm at once. Those desirous of the kingdom of Yoga, should take up the practice of hearing the anahata nada, with mind collected and free from all cares. Nada is the snare for catching the mind; and, when it is caught like a deer, it can be killed also like it. Nada is the bolt of the stable door for the horse (the mind of the Yogis). A Yogi should determine to practise constantly in the hearing of the nada sounds. The mercury of the Mind is deprived of its unsteadiness by being calcined with the sulphur of nada, and then it roams

---

16) Compare *Siva Samhita*, v, 22–30: "Let him close the ears with his thumbs, the eyes with index fingers, the nostrils with the middle fingers, and with the remaining four fingers let him press together the upper and lower lips. The Yogi, by having thus firmly confined the air, sees his soul in the shape of light. When one sees, without obstruction, this light for even a moment, becoming free from sin, he reaches the highest end. The Yogi, free from sin, and practising this continually, forgets his physical, subtle and causal bodies, and becomes one with that soul. He who practises this in secrecy, is absorbed in the Brahman, though he had been engaged in sinful works. This should be kept secret; it at once produces conviction; gives Nirvana to mankind. This is my most beloved Yoga. From practising this gradually, the Yogi begins to hear the mystic sounds (nadas). The first sound is like the hum of the honey-intoxicated bee, next that of a flute, then of a harp; after this, by the gradual practice of Yoga, the destroyer of the darkness of the world, he hears the sounds of ringing bells; then sounds like roar of thunder. When one fixes his full attention on this sound, being free from fear he gets absorption. O my beloved! When the mind of the Yogi is exceedingly engaged in this sound, he forgets all external things, and is absorbed in this sound. By this practice of Yoga he conquers all the three qualities (i.e. good, bad and indifferent); and being free from all states he is absorbed in Chidakasa (the ether of intelligence). There is no posture like that of Siddhasana, no power like that of Kumbha, no Mudra like the Khecari, and no absorption like that of Nada (the mystic sound)."

supportless in the akasa of Brahman. The mind is like a serpent; forgetting all its unsteadiness by hearing the nada, it does not run away anywhere. The fire, catching firewood, is extinguished along with it (after burning it up); and so the mind also, working with the nada, becomes latent along with it. The antahkarana (mind), like a deer, becomes absorbed and motionless on hearing the sound of bells, etc.; and then it is very easy for an expert archer to kill it.

The knowable interpenetrates the anahata sound which is heard, and the mind interpenetrates the knowable. The mind becomes absorbed there, which is the seat of the all pervading, almighty Lord. So long as the sounds continue, there is the idea of akasa. When they disappear, then it is called Para Brahman, Paramatman. Whatever is heard in the form of nada, is the sakti (power). That which is formless, the final state of the Tattvas, is the Paramesvara.[17]

---

17) *Hatha Yoga Pradipika*, iv, 79–101. Compare what is said about Raja Yoga in *Siva Samhita*, v, 158–82: "The Raja Yoga—By this knowledge the modifications of the mind are suspended, however active they may be: therefore, let the Yogi untiringly and unselfishly try to obtain this knowledge. When the modifications of the thinking principle are suspended, then one certainly becomes a Yogi; then is known the Indivisible, holy, pure Gnosis. Let him contemplate on his own reflection in the sky as beyond the Cosmic Egg: in the manner previously described. Through that let him think on the Great Void unceasingly. The Great Void, whose beginning is void, whose middle is void, whose end is void, has brilliancy of tens of millions of suns, and the coolness of tens of millions of moons. By contemplating continually on this, one obtains success. Let him practise daily this dhyana, within a year he shall obtain all success undoubtedly. He whose mind is absorbed in that place even for a second, is certainly a Yogi, and a good devotee, and is revered in all worlds. All his store of sins are at once verily destroyed. By seeing it one never returns to the path of this mortal universe; let the Yogi, therefore, practise this with great care by the path of Svadhisthana. I cannot describe the grandeur of this contemplation. He who practises, knows. He becomes respected by me. By meditation one at once knows the wonderful effects of this Yoga (i.e. of the contemplation of the void); undoubtedly he attains the psychic powers, called anima and laghima, etc. Thus have I described the Raja Yoga, it is kept secret in all the Tantras; now I shall describe to you briefly the Rajadhiraja Yoga.

"The Rajadhiraja Yoga:—Sitting in the Swastikasana, in a beautiful monastery, free from all men and animals having paid respects to his Guru, let the Yogi practise this contemplation. Knowing through the arguments of the Vedanta that the Jiva is independent and self-supported, let him make his mind also self-supported; and let him not contemplate on anything else. Undoubtedly, by this contemplation the highest success (Maha-siddhi) is obtained, by making the mind functionless; he himself becomes perfectly Full. He who practises this always, is the real passionless Yogi, he never uses the word 'I', but always finds himself full of atman. What is bondage, what is emancipation? To him ever all is One; undoubtedly, he who practises this always, is the really emancipated. He is the Yogi, he is the true devotee, he is worshipped in all the worlds, who contemplates the Jivatma and the Paramatma as related to each other as 'I' and 'I Am', who renounces 'I' and 'thou' and contemplates on the indivisible; the Yogi free from all attachments takes shelter in that contemplation in which, through the knowledge of superimposition and negation, all is dissolved. Leaving that Brahma, who is manifest, who is knowledge, who is bliss, and who is absolute consciousness, the deluded wander about, vainly discussing the manifested and the unmanifested. He who meditates on this movable and immovable universe, that is really unmanifest, but abandons the supreme Brahman—directly manifest—is verily absorbed in this universe. The Yogi, free from all attachment, constantly exerts

When I first learned of this particular technique, I tried it. By that time I had learned and practised all the physical techniques of Hatha Yoga and was well aware of the fact that no 'miracles' had transpired. On closing ears, eyes, nose, and lips, sounds were heard, but not as described in the text, and the mind did not become 'absorbed'. Aside from a high standard of physical well-being and the mental alertness and enthusiasm that attends such a condition, there was little perceptible change.

I had been told that the practices in and of themselves did not bestow any supernatural results. It was only when they were used in the proper sequence as prescribed by a guru that it would be possible to experience the psychological phenomena attributed to them. No amount of theorizing or study would help in this case. If I wanted to verify these claims, I would have to practise. The text says:

Whether young, old or too old, sick or lean, one who discards laziness, gets success if he practises Yoga. Success comes to him who is engaged in the practice; for by merely reading books on Yoga, one can never get success. Success cannot be attained by adopting a particular dress (Vesa). It cannot be gained by telling tales. Practice alone is the means of success. This is true, there is no doubt. Asanas (postures), various Kumbhakas, and other divine means, all should be practised in the practice of Hatha Yoga, till the fruit—Raja Yoga—is obtained.[18]

In order personally to experience the mental effects produced by the practice of Yoga, I underwent a three-month retreat, or intensified discipline. My training was directed and supervised by a well-trained Yogi at his hermitage. Such a discipline is of a highly personal nature

---

himself in keeping up this practice that leads to Gnosis, so that there may not be again the upheaval of Ignorance. The wise one, by restraining all his senses from their objects, and being free from all company, remains in the midst of these objects, as if in deep sleep, i.e. does not perceive them. Thus constantly practising the Self-luminous becomes manifest; here end all the teachings of the Guru, (they can help the student no further). Henceforth he must help himself, they can no more increase his reason or power, henceforth by the mere force of his own practice he must gain the Gnosis. That Gnosis from which the speech and mind turn back baffled, is only to be obtained through practice; for then this pure Gnosis bursts forth itself. The Hatha Yoga cannot be obtained without the Raja Yoga, nor can the Raja Yoga be attained without the Hatha Yoga. Therefore, let the Yogi first learn the Hatha Yoga from the instructions of the wise Guru. He who, while living in this physical body, does not practise Yoga is living merely for the sake of sensual enjoyment."

18) *Hatha Yoga Pradipika*, i, 66–9. Compare *Siva Samhita*, iii, 19: "Having received instructions in Yoga, and obtained a Guru who knows Yoga, let him practise with earnestness and faith, according to the method taught by the teachers."

and does not affect all alike; however, to enable others to learn what is required during a retreat and what the results were in my case, I shall briefly relate the general pattern. The reader will note that for the nada technique described in the text, my instructor substituted an analogous technique based on the theory of an inner light, instead of an inner sound. Otherwise the two techniques are similar in aim and structure.

The hermitage of my guru was surrounded by an extremely pictur-esque country-side; his dwelling was small, modest, and clean. Here he enjoyed the necessary isolation, yet the needs of life were readily accessible. I arrived in the early fall, which is considered one of the fa-vourable periods of the year to practise Yoga.[19] A small room had been

---

19) *Hatha Yoga Pradipika*, i. 12–14: "The Yogi should practise Hatha Yoga in a small room, four cubits square, situated in a solitary place, and free from stones, fire, water, and disturbances of all kinds, and in a country where justice is properly administered, where good people live, and food can be obtained easily and plentifully. The room should have a small door, be free from holes, hollows, and burrows, neither too high nor too low, well plastered with cow-dung and completely free from dirt and insects. The outside should be pleasant with bowers, a raised platform and a well, and surrounded with a wall. These characteristics of a room for Hatha Yoga have been described by adepts in the practice of Hatha. Having seated in such a room and free from all anxieties, he should only practise Yoga, as instructed by his Guru."

Compare *Gheranda Samhita*, v, 1–15: "Now I shall tell these the rules of Pranayama or regula-tion of breath. By its practice a man becomes godlike. (Four things are necessary in practising Pra-nayama). First, a good place; second, a suitable time; third, moderate food; and lastly, the purification of the nadis (Nerve vessels of the body).

"1. PLACE: The practice of Yoga should not be attempted in a far-off country (from home), nor in a forest, nor in a capital city, nor in the midst of a crowd. If one does so he does not achieve suc-cess. In a distant country one loses faith (because of the Yoga not being known there); in a forest one is without protection; and in the midst of a thick population, there is danger of exposure (for then the curious will trouble him). Therefore, let one avoid these three. In a good country whose king is just, where food is easily and abundantly procurable, where there are no disturbances, let one erect there a small hut, around it let him raise walls. And in the centre of the enclosure, let him sink a well and dig a tank. Let the hut be neither very high nor very low; let it be free from insects. It should be completely smeared over with cow dung. In a hut thus built and situated in such a hidden place, let him practise Pranayama.

"2. TIME: The practice of Yoga should not be commenced in these four seasons out of six: hemanta (winter), sisira (cold), grisma (hot), varsa (rainy). If one begins in these seasons, one will contract diseases. The practice of Yoga should be commenced by a beginner in spring (vasanta); and autumn (sarad). By so doing, he attains success; and verily he does not become liable to diseases. The six seasons occur in their order in the twelve months beginning with Caitra and ending with Phalguna: two months being occupied by each season. But each season is experienced for four months, beginning with Magha and ending with Phalguna. The six seasons are as follows:

SEASONS	MONTHS (SANSKRIT)	ENGLISH
Vasanta or Spring	Caitra and Vaisakha	Mar., Apr.
Grisma or Summer	Jyestha and Asadha	May. June
Varsa or Rainy	Sravana and Bhadra	July, Aug.

set aside for me near the family compound of his patron. My teacher lived a regulated life, so I was obliged to wait for the appointed hour in the afternoon which he had set aside for receiving visits in order to pay my first respects. The formalities were simple, but fitting. He was seated on a raised wooden bench covered with a tiger skin. This is where he practised and slept. There was a small grass mat on the earthen floor where I sat. He could speak no English, so it was necessary to have an interpreter. A young Brahmin student who was studying with him served in this capacity. There was no 'mystical laying on of hands' or other religious ceremony. Aside from his interest in my well-being, he confined this visit as well as others that followed to training and to philosophical conversation. He expressed willingness to answer all my questions and was ever ready to help me with problems as they arose.

The members of the family living in the compound knew that I had come to practise Yoga; every consideration was given me. I was not to be disturbed for any reason. Certain hours were established when they could come to the quarters I was using, and certain individuals were appointed to look after me. Most important was the man who was to prepare my food. In this respect, also, I was extremely fortunate in having the young Brahmin student of my guru take care of me. He was familiar with all the restrictions in diet and knew what was needed.[20]

Sarad or Autumn	Asvina and Karttika	Sept., Oct.
Hemanta or Winter	Agrahayana and Pausa	Nov., Dec.
Sisira or Cold	Magha and Phalguna	Jan., Feb.

"Now I shall tell thee the experiencing of seasons. They are as follows:

BEGINNING FROM ENDING WITH	SEASON	ENGLISH
Magha to Vaisakha	Vasantanubhava	Jan. to Apr.
Caitra to Asadha	Grismanubhava	Mar. to June
Asadha to Asvina	Varsanubhava	June to Sept.
Bhadra to Agrahayana	Saradnubhava	Aug. to Nov.
Karttika to Magha	Hemantanubhava	Oct. to Jan.
Agrahayana to Phalguna	Sisiranubhava	Nov. to Feb.

"The practice of Yoga should be commenced either in Vasanta (spring) or Sarad (autumn). For in these seasons success is attained without much trouble."

20) Injurious and recommended foods and conduct for the practice of Yoga are given. *Hatha Yoga Pradipika*, i, 61–5: "Food Injurious to a Yogi; Bitter, sour, saltish, hot, green vegetables, fermented, oily, mixed with til seed, rape seed, intoxicating liquors, fish, meat, curds, chhaasa pulses, plums, oil cake, asafoetida (hingu), garlic, onion, etc. should not be eaten. Food heated again, dry, having too much salt, sour, minor grains, and vegetables that cause burning sensation, should not be eaten.

"Fire, women, travelling, etc. should be avoided. As said by Goraksa, one should keep aloof from the society of the evil-minded, fire, women, travelling, early morning bath, fasting and all kinds of bodily exertion.

"Wheat, rice, barley, sastika (a kind of rice), good corns, milk, ghee, sugar, butter, sugar candy, honey, dried ginger, Parwal (a vegetable), the five vegetables, moong, pure water, these are very beneficial to those who practise Yoga. A Yogi should eat tonics (things giving strength), well sweetened, greasy (made with ghee), milk, butter, etc., which may increase humours of the body, according to his desires." To understand these requirements it is necessary to study the Indian medical work Susruta.

Compare *Gheranda Samhita*, v, 16–32: "He who practices Yoga without moderation of diet, incurs various disease, and obtains no success. A Yogin should eat rice, barley (bread), or wheaten bread. He may eat Mudga beans (Phaseolus mungo), Masa beans (Phaseolus radiatus), gram, etc. These should be clean, white, and free from chaff. A Yogin my eat patola (a kind of cucumber), jackfruit, manakacu (Arum Colocasia), kakkola (a kind of berry), the jujube, the bonduc nut (Bonducella guilandine), cucumber, plantain, fig; the unripe plantain, the small plantain, the plantain stem, and roots, brinjal, and medicinal roots and fruits (e.g. rhhi, etc.). He may eat green, fresh vegetables, black vegetables, the leaves of patola, and Vastuka, the hima-locika. These are the five sakas (vegetable leaves) praised as fit food for Yogins. Pure, sweet and cooling food should be eaten to fill half the stomach; eating thus sweet juices with pleasure, and leaving the other half of the stomach empty is called moderation in diet. Half the stomach should be filled with food, one quarter with water; and one quarter should be kept empty for practising pranayama.

"Prohibited Foods: In the beginning of Yoga practice one should discard bitter, acid, salt, pungent and roasted things, curd, whey, heavy vegetables, wine, palm nuts, and overripe jack-fruit. So also kulattha and masur beans, pandu fruit, pumpkins and vegetable stems, gourds, berries, kathabel, (feronis elephantum), kanta-bilva and palasa (Butea frondosa). So also kadamba (Naucles cadamba), jambira (citron), bimba, lakuca (a kind of bread fruit tree), onions, lotus, Kamaranga, piyala (Buchananis latifolia), hingu (asafoetida), salmali, kemuka.

"A beginner should avoid much travelling, company of women, and warming himself by fire. So also he should avoid fresh butter, ghee, thickened milk, sugar, and date-sugar, etc., as well as ripe plantain, coco-nut, pomegranate, dates, lavani fruit, amlaki (myrobalans), and everything containing acid juices. But cardamom, jaiphal, clove, aphrodisiacs, or stimulants, the rose-apple, haritaki, and palm dates, a Yogin may eat while practising Yoga. Easily digestible, agreeable and cooling foods which nourish the elements of the body, a Yogin may eat according to his desire. But a Yogin should avoid hard (not easily digestible), sinful, or putrid, very hot, or very stale, as well as very cooling or very much exciting food. He should avoid early morning (before sunrise) baths, fasting, etc., or anything giving pain to the body: so also is prohibited to him eating only once a day or not eating at all. But he may remain without food for three hours. Regulating his life in this way, let him practise Pranayama. In the beginning before commencing it, he should take a little milk and ghee daily, and take his food twice daily, once at noon and once in the evening."

Compare *Siva Samhita*, iii, 33–8: "The Yogi should renounce, the following:—1. Acids; 2. astringents; 3. pungent substances; 4. salt; 5. mustard; 6. bitter things; 7. much walking; 8. early bathing (before sunrise); and 9. things roasted in oil; 10. theft; 11. killing (of animals); 12. enmity towards any person; 13. pride; 14. duplicity; and 15. crookedness; 16. fasting; 17. untruth; 18. thoughts other than those of moksa; 19. cruelty towards animals; 20. companionship of women; 21. worship of (or handling or sitting near) fire; and 22. much talking without regard to pleasantness or unpleasantness of speech; and lastly, 23. much eating.

"Now I will tell you the means by which success in Yoga is quickly obtained; it must be kept secret by the practitioner so that success may come with certainty. The great Yogi should observe always the following observances: —He should use 1. clarified butter; 2. milk: 3. sweet food; and 4. betel without lime; 5. camphor; 6. kind words; 7. pleasant monastery or retired cell, having a small door; 8. hear discourses on truth; and 9. always discharge his household duties with Vairagya (without attachment); 10. sing the name of Visnu; 11. and hear sweet music; 12. patience, 13. constancy;

I did not have to give my diet a thought, but could devote all my time to my discipline, taking whatever was provided at the fixed hour.

The first three weeks were given to purifying and strengthening my system so that I could carry the practice of pranayama to a point where I could experience some of its effects. Each morning I arose at 4 a.m. and thoroughly cleansed the system by doing dhauti,[21] neti,[22] and basti.[23] After which I did uddiyana[24] and nauli.[25] These two practices I had been doing daily for purposes of general health, and it was therefore no problem to bring them up to the maximum number of repetitions. Then followed the head stand,[26] starting with half an hour. The next practice was bhastrika.[27] I started with one minute at the rate of about one hundred strokes per minute and then suspended for one minute, after which I exhaled slowly and rested for thirty seconds before starting the next round. Each week I increased the suspension one minute. Ten rounds of this concluded my morning practice.

Before my food arrived I usually took a short stroll. Until it was time to resume my practice again at ten-thirty, I devoted my energies to the many studies that had been assigned to me. I began the midday routine with the head stand for another thirty-minute period, and then I performed ten routines of bhastrika, as I have already described. The

---

14. forgiveness; 15. austerities; 16. purifications; 17. modesty; 18. devotion; and 19. service of the Guru.

"When the air enters the sun, it is the proper time for the Yogi to take his food (i.e. when the breath flows through the Pingala); when the air enters the moon, he should go to sleep (i.e. when the breath flows through the left nostril or the Ida). Yoga Pranayama) should not be practised just after the meals, nor when one is very hungry; before beginning the practice, some milk and butter should be taken. When one is well established in his practice, then he need not observe these restrictions. The practitioner should eat in small quantities at a time though frequently; and should practise Kumbhaka daily at the stated times."

21) See above, pp. 34–37.

22) *Ibid.*, p. 40 ff.

23) *Ibid.*, p. 37–38.

24) *Ibid.*, pp. 42–47

25) *Ibid.*, p. 45.

26) See above, p. 28.

27) *Ibid.*, p. 45–47.

rest of the period was devoted to developing the asanas.[28] This is common practice of Yogis in order to introduce a little variety into their regime. My principal meal was brought after this period.

Until four o'clock I rested and read. The afternoon routine started with uddiyana and nauli; then the head stand for thirty minutes and another ten rounds of bhastrika. I added more time to the head stand each week, until I finally brought it up to one hour for each practice period. In addition I increased the bhastrika one minute each week, until I could do it at the rate of 120 strokes per minute for three continuous minutes. This was my limit. The suspension I continued to increase until I could continue it for five minutes and dispense with the rest of a few seconds between rounds.

In preparation for practising contemplation, my teacher recommended what is commonly known as the 'candle exercise', which I was to use every evening before retiring.[29] It is a simple technique for

---

28)   *Ibid.*, p. 19–25.

29)   Three different forms of contemplation are discussed in *Gheranda Samhita*, vi, 1–22: "The Dhyana or contemplation is of three sorts: gross, luminous and subtle. When a particular figure (such as one's Guru or Deity), is contemplated on, it is Sthula or gross contemplation. When Brahman or Prakrti is contemplated on as a mass of light, it is called Jyotis-contemplation. When Brahman as Bindu (pont) and Kundali force is contemplated on, it is Suksma or Subtle contemplation."

"1. Sthula Dhyana: (Having closed the eyes), let him contemplate that there is a sea of nectar in the region of his heart: that in the midst of that sea an island of precious stones, the very sand of which is pulverized diamonds and rubies. That on all sides of it, Kadamba trees, laden with sweet flowers; that, next to those trees, like a rampart, a row of flowering trees, such as malati, mallika, jati, kesara, campaka, parijata and padma, and that the fragrance of these flowers is spread all round, in every quarter. In the middle of this garden, let the Yogin imagine that there stands a beautiful Kalpa tree, having four branches, representing the four Vedas, and that it is full of flowers and fruits. Beatles are humming there and cuckoos singing. Beneath that tree let him imagine a rich platform of precious gems, and on that a costly throne inlaid with jewels, and that on that throne sits his particular Deity as taught to him by his Guru. Let him contemplate on the appropriate form, ornaments and vehicle of that Deity. The constant contemplation of such a form is Sthula Dhyana.

"Another Process:—Let the Yogin imagine that in the pericarp of the great thousand-petalled Lotus (Brain) there is a smaller lotus having twelve petals. Its colour is white, highly luminous, having twelve bija letters, named ha, sa, ksa, ma, la va, ra, yum, ha, sa, kha, phrem. In the pericarp of this smaller lotus there are three lines forming a triangle, a, ka, tha; having three angles called ha, la, ksa: and in the middle of this triangle, there is the Pranava Om. Then let him contemplate that in that there is a beautiful seat having Nada and Bindu. On that seat there are two swans, and a pair of wooden sandals. There let him contemplate his Guru Deva, having two arms and three eyes, and dressed in pure white, anointed with white sandal-paste, wearing garlands of white flowers; to the left of whom stands Sakti of blood-red colour. By thus contemplating the Guru, the Sthula Dhyana is attained

"2. Jyotirdhyana: I have told thee of the Sthula Dhyana; listen now to the contemplation of Light, by which the Yogin attains success and sees his Self. In the Muladhara is Kundalini of the form

establishing an afterimage on the retina, which you are supposed to watch with fixed attention until it disappears. Place a lighted candle some eighteen inches in front of you on a level with your eyes and stare at the flame until tears begin to flow. Then close your eyes with cupped hands and watch the mental image. The problem is to try to hold the image still. It is permissible to move it backward and forward, but it must not be allowed to move sideways or up and down. The reason for using this practice is due to the similarity between the afterimage thus produced and the 'light of the body' in Yogic theory. Eventually a similar light is supposed to appear without the aid of the candle. Instead of working with the sounds in the body, as the text advocated, my teacher preferred to concentrate the mind on the lights within the body.[30]

During the first month the emphasis was placed on the physical aspect of the training, without concern about the mind. I was told that until the breath suspension had been developed to at least three minutes nothing of any significance could be done. The ultimate aim is to make the mind a blank so that the bodily lights will appear. To prepare for this I was taught a simple technique. The eyes are rolled back in the

---

of a serpent. The Jivatman is there like the flame of a lamp. Contemplate on this flame as the Luminous Brahman. This is the Tejodhyana or Jyotirdhana,

"Another Process: In the middle of the eyebrows, above the Manas, there is the Light of Om. Let him contemplate on this flame. This is another method of contemplation of Light.

"3. Suksma Dhyana: O Canda! thou hast heard the Tejodhyana, listen now to the Suksma Dhyana. When by a great good fortune, the Kundalini is awakened, it joins with the Atman and leaves the body through the portals of the eyes; and enjoys itself by walking in the royal road. It cannot be seen on account of its subtleness and great changeability. The Yogin, however, attains this success by performing Sambhavi Mudra, i.e. by gazing fixedly at space without winking. (Then he will see his Suksma Sarira.) This is called Suksma Dhyana, difficult to be attained even by the Devas, as it is a great mystery.

"The contemplation on Light is a hundred times superior to contemplation on Form; and a hundred thousand times superior to Tejodhyana is the contemplation of the Suksma. O Canda! thus have I told thee Dhyana Yoga—a most precious knowledge; for, by it, there is direct perception of the Self. Hence Dhyana is belauded."

30) *Siva Samhita*, v. 22–6: "Let him close the ears with his thumbs, the eyes with index fingers, the nostrils with the middle fingers, and with the remaining four fingers let him press together the upper and lower lips. The Yogi, by having thus firmly confined the air, sees his soul in the shape of light. When one sees, without obstruction, this light even a moment, becoming free from sin, he reaches the highest end. The Yogi, free from sin, and practising this continually, forgets his physical, subtle, and causal bodies, and becomes one with that soul. He who practises this in secrecy, is absorbed in the Brahman, though he had been engaged in sinful works. This should be kept secret; it at once produces conviction; it gives Nirvana to mankind. This is my most beloved Yoga. From practising this gradually, the Yogi begins to hear the mystic sounds (nadas)."

head, letting the lids find a restful position, usually slightly open and showing a little of the whites of the eyes. The mind is concentrated on the space between the eyebrows.[31] After a time this became a simple and comfortable position for the eyes and the mind.

In the second month the lights made their appearance. In the beginning it was not unlike looking into a kaleidoscope; but this condition soon passed, and single colours, brilliant and radiant, remained.[32] Then came the 'white light' that is referred to so frequently. This was an interesting phenomenon. At times it became almost blinding; however, it never lasted long. This was the first step. I was taught to work with this light by watching it and trying to hold it, but it would vanish as mysteriously as it appeared. This was not the Kundalini light, I was told. Taking an analogy from nature, my teacher told me that this light was comparable to the flare of soft light of static electricity seen during thunderstorms on the desert, while Kundalini light was equivalent to the lightning itself and would appear in a similar fashion.

A technique for inducing these lights to appear at will was given to me. It is called Sambhavi mudra. This method is described in the text.

The Vedas and the Sastras are like ordinary public women. Sambhavi Mudra is the one, which is secluded like a respectable lady. Aiming at Brahman inwardly, while keeping the sight directed to the external objects, without blinking the eyes, is called the Sambhavi Mudra, hidden in the Vedas and the Sastras. When the Yogi remains inwardly attentive to Brahman, keeping the mind and the Prana absorbed, and the sight steady, as if seeing everything while in reality seeing nothing outside, below, or above, verily then it is called Sambhavi Mudra, which is learnt by the favour of a Guru. In this condition takes place the manifestation of that great Sambhu (Siva) tattva [essence] which is neither Sunya nor Asunya

---

31) Compare *Hatha Yoga Pradipika*, iv, 38: "Fix the gaze on the light (seen on the tip of the nose) and raise the eyebrows a little, with the mind contemplating as before (in the Sambhavi Mudra, that is, inwardly thinking of Brahman, but apparently looking outside). This will create the Unman Avastha at once." See also 39–40: "Some are devoted to the Vedas, some to a Nigama, while others are enwrapt in Logic, but none knows the value of the Taraka Mudra, which enables one to cross the ocean of existence. With steady calm mind and half closed eyes, fixed on the tip of the nose, stopping the Ida and the Pingala without blinking, he who can see the light which is the all, the seed, the entire, brilliant, great Tattvam, approaches Him, who is the great object. What is the use of more talk?"

32) The colours of the lights that appeared were blue, yellow, red and white.

[void nor non-void].[33]

By using this technique I was eventually able to see this white light with my eyes wide open in the daylight. The mind seemed to be wiped out completely and nothing existed but this brilliant light. After a time it became no problem to make it appear at will, whether sitting or walking about. I frequently did so when on my morning stroll.[34] Another practice recommended for producing this effect which I have found successful is known as the 'Shadow Man'.

These lights are called 'tattvic lights' and are said to represent the energies flowing through their respective nerve centres, which are known as chakras.[35] In time, they say, it is possible to gain such control over the nervous system that any desired light can be made to appear and remain for a definite length of time. Control is established by making first one and then another stay for not less than an hour. Eventually, one works only with the white light, and in this way the Kundalini light is made to appear. To help bring about the manifestation of the Kundalini light the various mudras I have described are used.

At this stage the mental aspect of Yoga is stressed and the different techniques for enabling the mind to become absorbed in the light are

33) *Hatha Yoga Pradipika*, iv. 34–6. Compare *Gheranda Samhita*, iii, 64–7: "Fixing the gaze between the eyebrows, behold the Self-existent. This is Sambhavi, secret in all the Tantras. The Vedas, the scriptures, the Puranas are like public women, but this Sambhavi should be guarded as if it were a lady of a respectable family. He, who knows this Sambhavi, is like the Adinatha, he is Narayana, he is Brahma, the Creator. Mahesvara has said, Truly, truly, and again truly, he who knows, the Sambhavi, is Brahman. There is no doubt of this"

34) See *Siva Samhita*, v, 15–21: "The invocation of Pratika (shadow) gives to the devotee the objects seen as well as unseen; undoubtedly, by its very sight, a man becomes pure. In a clear sun-lit sky behold with a steady gaze your own divine reflection; whenever this is seen even for a single second in the sky, you behold God at once in the sky. He who daily sees his shadow in the sky will get his years increased and will never die an accidental death. When the shadow is seen fully reflected in the field of the sky, then he obtains victory; and conquering the vayu, he goes everywhere.
"How to invoke: At the time of the rising sun, or by moon, let him steadily fix his gaze on the neck of the shadow he throws; then after some time, let him look into the sky; if he sees a full grey shadow in the sky, it is auspicious. He who always practises this and knows the Paramatma, becomes fully happy, through the grace of his shadow. At the time of commencing travel, marriage, or auspicious work, or when in trouble, it is of great use. This invocation of the shadow destroys sins and increases virtue. By practising it always, he begins at last to see it in his heart, and the persevering Yogi gets liberation."

35) See *Serpent Power*, by Arthur Avalon, for full treatment of this subject—the chapter on the 'Centres'.

used. One method is a series of mental mudras known as 'dharanas',[36]

---

36)   They are described in *Gheranda Samhita*, iii, 68–81: "The Sambhavi has been explained:
hear now the five Dharanas. Learning these five Dharanas, what cannot be accomplished in this
world? By this human body one can visit and revisit Svargaloka, he can go wherever he likes, as swift-
ly as mind, he acquires the faculty of moving in the air. [These five Dharanas are: Parthivi (Earthy),
Ambhasi (Watery), Vayavi (Aerial), Agneyi (Fiery) and Akasi (Ethereal).]

"PARTHIVI: The Parthivi-Tattva has the colour of orpiment (yellow), the letter 'la' is its secret
symbol or seed, its form is four-sided, and Brahma, its presiding deity. Place this Tattva in the heart,
and fix by Kumbhaka the Prana-Vayus and the Citta there for the period of five ghatikas (2 ½ hours).
This is called Adho-dharana. By this, one conquers the Earth, and no earthy-elements can injure him;
and it causes steadiness. He who practises daily this dharana becomes like the conqueror of Death;
as an Adept he walks this earth.

"AMBHASI: The Water-Tattva is white like the Kunda-flower or a conch or the moon, its form is
circular like the moon, the letter va is the seed of this ambrosial element, and Visnu is its presiding
deity. By Yoga, produce the water-tattva in the heart, and fix there the Prana with the Citta (consciousness), for five ghatikas, practising kumbhaka. This is Watery Dharana; it is the destroyer of all
sorrows. Water cannot injure him who practises this. The Ambhasi is a great mudra; the Yogin who
knows it never meets death even in the deepest water. This should be kept carefully concealed. By
revealing it success is lost, verily I tell you the truth.

"AGNEYI: The Fire-tattva is situated at the navel, its colour is red like the Indra-gopa insect, its
form is triangular, its seed is ra, its presiding deity is Rudra. It is refulgent like the sun, and the giver of
success. Fix the Prana along with the Citta on this Tattva for five ghatikas. This is called Fire-dharana,
destroyer of the fear of dreadful death, and fire cannot injure him. Even if the practitioner is thrown
into burning fire, by virtue of this Mudra he remains alive, without fear of death.

"VAYAVI: The Air-tattva is black as unguent for the eyes (collirium), the letter ya is its seed,
and Isvara its presiding deity. This Tattva is full of Sattva quality. Fix the Prana and the Citta for five
ghatikas on this Tattva. This is Vayavi-dharana. By this, the practitioner walks in the air. This should
not be taught to the wicked or to those devoid of faith. By so doing success is lost. O Canda! this is
verily the truth.

"AKASI DHARANA: The Akasa-tattva has the colour of pure sea-water, 'ha' is its seed, its presiding deity is Sadasiva. Fix the Prana along with Citta for five ghatikas in this tattva. This is Ether-dha-
rana. It opens the gates of emancipation. He who knows this Dharana is the real Yogin. Death and
old age do not approach him, nor does he perish at the Pralaya [dissolution of the Universe at the
end of a world period]."

Compare *Siva Samhita*, v, 43–51: "(Various kinds of Dharana.) Let the Yogi seat himself in the
Padmasana and fix his attention on the cavity of the throat, let him place his tongue at the base
of the palate; by this he will extinguish hunger and thirst. Below the cavity of the throat, there is a
beautiful Nadi (vessel) called Kurma; when the Yogi fixes his attention on it, he acquires great concentration of the thinking principle (chitta). When the Yogi constantly thinks that he has got a third
eye–the eye of Siva—in the middle of his forehead, he then perceives a fire brilliant like lightning.
By contemplating on this light, all sins are destroyed, and even the most wicked person obtains the
highest end. If the experienced Yogi thinks of this light day and night he sees Siddhas (adepts), and
can certainly converse with them. He who contemplates on Sunya (void or vacuum or space), while
walking or standing dreaming or waking, becomes altogether ethereal and is absorbed in the Chid
Akasa. The Yogi, desirous of success, should always obtain this knowledge; by habitual exercise he
becomes equal to me; through the force of this knowledge he becomes the beloved of all. Having
conquered all the elements and being void of all hopes and worldly connections, when the Yogi sitting in the Padmasana, fixes his gaze on the tip of his nose, his mind becomes dead and he obtains
the spiritual power called Khecari. The great Yogi beholds light, pure as holy mountain (Kailas), and

which are ways of concentrating the mind, frequently used in conjunction with rites and rituals in order to help produce the highest possible degree of mental abstraction.

My retreat concluded with a ceremony that occasionally is employed to establish fully the inner experience of absorbing the mind in these lights, a ceremony which therefore bears some relation to the dharanas. The particulars of this ceremony, though not important for the Yogi, may be of interest to the occidental reader. I was interested in this particular rite, for I had heard about it. My teacher was well trained in the techniques of putting on various rituals and was gracious enough to give me the opportunity of undergoing the experience. Generally Yogis do not advocate such measures; however, they say that they are all right for those who do not have the capacity to practise Yoga. During the early years of my teacher's training he had passed through a period when he was a devoted follower of rites and rituals, but later he found a teacher who led him out of this 'spiritual cul-de-sac'. Since then he has had no use for them except to conduct them for a student from time to time. But he made it clear that no amount of ceremony can awaken Kundalini. All experiences resulting from such practices are purely mental, not actual, while the arousing of Kundalini is believed to bring about an actual physiological change in the body.

In preparation for the ceremony I fasted for twenty-four hours and directed my meditations toward preparing my mind. At 10 p.m. I began the preliminary worship intended fully to awaken the heart. Before entering the shrine I took a bath as part of the purification rites. Just outside the entrance I made my oblation of humility and drew on the ground a triangle, a circle, and a square, one inside the other. In the centre I placed my vessel of consecrated water and worshipped the fire, the sun, and the moon by throwing perfume and scented flowers into the water while repeating the mantras that had been given to me and making various gestures with my hands. These formations of the hands are called 'mudras' and are symbolic of various attitudes of mind, not to be confused with the practices known by this name. All ritual details had been given to me on previous occasions.

Stepping across the sacred threshold with my left foot, I lightly

through the force of his exercise in it, he becomes the lord and guardian of the light. Stretching himself on the ground, let him contemplate on this light; by so doing all his weariness and fatigue are destroyed. By contemplating on the back part of his head, he becomes the conqueror of death."

struck the doorway with my left shoulder. First I worshipped before the presiding deity. At the place reserved for me I sprinkled the ground with water and did trataka[37] while repeating mantras. Before taking my seat I sprinkled water to remove all celestial obstacles and struck the ground three times with my heel to remove the obstacles of the earth. Burning incense of sandal wood, saffron, and camphor, I marked off a rectangular space for my seat within which I drew a triangle and then covered it with my mat. Assuming the padmasana posture, I sat facing north. Throughout these preliminary rites my guru sat motionless, repeating mantras.[38]

---

37)   See above, p. 33 *n.*

38)   The emphasis placed on mantras by some schools of thought is expressed in Siva Samhita, v, 188–204: "Now shall I tell you the best of practices, the Japa [repetition] of Mantra: from this one gains happiness in this as well in the world beyond this. By knowing this highest of the Mantras, the Yogi certainly attains success (Siddhi): this gives all power and pleasure to the one-pointed Yogi. In the four-petalled Muladhara lotus is the bija [seed] of speech, brilliant as lightning (i.e. the syllable Aim). In the heart is the bija of love, beautiful as the Bandhuka ower (klim). In the space between the two eyebrows (i.e. in the Ajna lotus), is the bija of Sakti (strim), brilliant as tens of millions of moons. These three seeds should be kept secret—they give enjoyment and emancipation. Let the Yogi repeat these three Mantras and try to attain success. Let him learn this Mantra from his Guru, let him repeat it neither too fast nor too slowly, keeping the mind free from all doubts, and understanding the mystic relation between the letters of the Mantra. The wise Yogi, intently fixing his attention on this Mantra, performing all the duties peculiar to his caste, should perform one hundred thousand Homas (fire sacrifices), and then repeat this Mantra three hundred thousand times in the presence of the Goddess Tripura. At the end of this sacred repetition (Japa) let the wise Yogi again perform Homa, in a triangular hollow, with sugar, milk, butter and the flower of Karavi (oleander). By this performance of Homa-Japa-Homa, the Goddess Tripura Bhairavi, who has been propitiated by the above Mantra, becomes pleased, and grants all the desires of the Yogi. Having satisfied the Guru and having received this highest of Mantra, in the proper way, and performing its repetition in the way laid down, with mind concentrated, even the most heavy-burdened with past Karmas attains success. The Yogi, who having controlled his senses, repeats this Mantra one hundred thousand times, gains the power of attracting others. By repeating it two lacs [two hundred thousand] of times he can control all persons—they come to him as freely as women go to a pilgrimage. They give him all that they possess, and remain always under his control. By repeating this Mantra three lacs of times, all the deities presiding over the spheres as well as the sphere are brought under his dominion. By repeating it six lacs of times, he becomes the vehicle of power—yea, the protector of the world—surrounded by servants. By repeating this twelve lacs of times, the lords of Yaksas, Raksas and the Nagas come under his control; all obey his command constantly. By repeating this fifteen lacs of times, the Siddhas, the Vidyadharas, the Gandharvas, the Apsaras come under the control of the Yogi. There is no doubt of it. He attains immediately the knowledge of all audition and thus all-knowing hood. By repeating this eighteen lacs of times, he, in this body can rise from the ground; he attains verily the luminous body; he goes all over the universe, wherever he likes; he sees the pores of the earth, i.e., he sees the interspaces and the molecules of this solid earth. By repeating this twenty-eight lacs of times, he becomes the lord of the Vidyadharas, the wise Yogi becomes Kamarupi (i.e., can assume whatever from he desires). By repeating these thirty lacs of times, he becomes equal to Brahma and Visnu. He becomes a Rudra, by sixty lac repetitions, by eighty lac repetitions, he becomes all-enjoyer,

The offering which I was to make to the deity symbolically residing within my heart had to be purified. This was done by reciting mantras over it seven times, while making various gestures with my hands. Before drinking it, I had to recite mantras in praise of Kundalini. After drinking it, I bowed to my guru by placing my folded hands first on my left ear, then on my right ear, and finally on the middle of my forehead, after which I sat for a few minutes in silent meditation. Placing the articles of worship on my right side and the wine on my left, I encircled myself with water. For further protection from malignant spirits, I mentally surrounded myself with a wall of symbolic fire. Then I purified the palms of my hands by rubbing between them a flower that had been dipped in sandal paste. To dispose of it, I threw it over my left shoulder. The last act of protection against evil spirits was to snap the fingers of my right hand in the palm of my left hand toward each of the four directions.

The principal object of this ceremony is to follow mentally the cosmic pattern for the dissolution[39] of the elements of the human constituent until the mind becomes absorbed in what is known to them

by repeating one ten of millions of times, the great Yogi is absorbed in the Parama Brahman. Such a practitioner is hardly to be found throughout the three worlds."

39)   The absorption of the different elements is treated in *Siva Samhita*, i, 78–88: "The earth becomes subtle and is dissolved in water; water is resolved into fire; fire similarly merges in air; [sic] gets absorption in ether, and ether is resolved in Avidya (Ignorance), air which merges into the Great Brahma. There are two forces—Viksepa (the out-going energy), and Avarana (the transforming energy) which are of great potentiality and power, and whose form is happiness. The great Maya, when non-intelligent and material, has three attributes Sattva (rhythm) Rajas (energy) and Tamas (inertia). The non-intelligent form of Maya covered by the Avarana force (concealment), manifests itself as the universe, owing to the nature of Viksepa force. When the Avidya has an excess of Tamas, then it manifests itself as Durga; the intelligence which presides over her is called Isvara. When the Avidya has an excess of Sattva it manifests itself as the beautiful Lakshmi; the Intelligence which presides over her is called Visnu. When the Avidya has an excess of Rajas, it manifests itself as the wise Saraswati; the intelligence which presides over her is known as Brahma. Gods like Siva, Brahma, Visnu, etc., are all seen in the great Spirit; bodies and all material objects are the various products of Avidya. The wise have thus explained the creation of the world—Tattwas (elements) and Not-Tattwas (non-elements) are thus produced—not otherwise. All things are seen as finite, etc. (endowed with qualities, etc.), and there arise various distinctions merely through words and names; but there is no real difference. Therefore, the things do not exist; the great and glorious One that manifests them, alone exists; though things are false and unreal, yet, as the reflection of the real, they, for the time being, appear real. The One Entity, blissful, entire and all-pervading, alone exists, and nothing else; he who constantly realises this knowledge is freed from death and the sorrow of the world-wheel. When, through the knowledge that all is illusory perception (Aropa) and by intellectual refutation (Apavada) of other doctrines, this universe is resolved into the one, the, there exists that One and nothing else; then this is clearly perceived by the mind."

as the 'universal principle of intelligence'. This is supposed to simulate the process that takes place at death. It is believed that if an individual can gain sufficient control over the subtle forces of his nature to enable him actually to regulate the movement of these elements revealed by the different lights that appear before the mind when the eyes are closed that he can 'conquer death'.

In order to aid this process of cosmic dissolution, I had been instructed mentally to awaken the Kundalini force by practising pranayama while my teacher was reciting mantras designed to aid my imagination. During each suspension I mentally went through the process of awakening this latent force and leading it through the respective centres until it became united with the universal consciousness. At each stage the emotional experience became more intensified, until finally I completely lost awareness of all external surroundings and with my eyes wide open could see nothing but a brilliant light. An ecstatic condition ensued that is difficult to describe. Finally a climax was reached, and the trance began to subside slowly, and ordinary consciousness returned. The last stage was to reverse the process—mentally to unfold the individual entity along the lines of cosmic creation[40] and return the Kundalini force to its seat at the base of the spine. The entire experience was mental and had nothing to do with samadhi which is the phenomenon that occurs when Kundalini is actually awakened. It was a state of mind created by ceremony;[41] I was told that to attain the ultimate god of samadhi I should have to

---

40) The order of cosmic creation is discussed in *Siva Samhita,* i, 69—77: "The Lord willed to create his creatures; from His will came out Avidya (Ignorance), the mother of this false universe. There takes place the conjunction between the Pure Brahma and Avidya, from which arises Brahma, from which comes out the Akasa. From the Akasa emanated the air; from air came the fire; from fire—water; and from water came the earth. This is the order of subtle emanation. From ether, air; from the air and ether combined came fire; from the triple compound of ether, air and fire came water; and from the combination of ether, air, fire, and water was produced the (gross) earth. The quality of ether is sound; of air motion and touch. Form is the quality of fire, and taste of water. And smell is the quality of the earth. There is no gainsaying this. Akasa has one quality; air two, fire three, water four, and earth five qualities, viz—sound, touch, taste, form and smell. This has been declared by the wise. Form is perceived through the eyes, smell through the nose, taste through the tongue, touch through the skin and sound through the ear. These are verily the organs of perception. From Intelligence has come out all this universe, movable and immovable; whether or not its existence can be inferred, the 'All Intelligence' One does exist."

41) For a more comprehensive discussion of tantrik rituals see the works of Sir John Woodroffe (Arthur Avalon), *The Principles of Tantra*, Vols. 1–11, "The Great Liberation," "Shakti and Shakta," and 'The Garland of Letters."

continue my Yoga practices.

It is a popular misconception that in order to practise Yoga one must 'leave the world' and live in a hidden sanctuary, isolated from all human intercourse. The Siva Samhita concludes with the following statement.

Therefore, the Yogis should perform Yoga according to the rules of practice. He who is contented with what he gets, who restrains his senses, being a householder, who is not absorbed in the household duties, certainly attains emancipation by the practice of Yoga. Even the lordly householders obtain success by Japa, if they perform the duties of Yoga properly. Let, therefore, a householder also exert in Yoga (his wealth and conditions of life are no obstacles in this). Living in the house amidst wife and children, but being free from attachment to them, practising Yoga in secrecy, a householder even finds marks of success (slowly crowning his efforts), and thus following this teaching of mine, he ever lives in blissful happiness.[42]

The text, however, points out the desirability of keeping one's effort a private matter, for Yoga was never intended for the parlour. "The Yogi desirous of success, should keep the Hatha Yoga as a great secret. It becomes fruitful while kept secret, revealed it loses its power."[43]

Any conclusions that I might draw from my experiences would necessarily be tentative, but they are, in any case, no legitimate part of this report. However, I must say again that during my studies of the science of Yoga I found that it holds no magic, performs no miracles, and reveals nothing supernatural. I was directed at every stage to practice if I wanted to know its secrets; so I can do no better, in closing, than to repeat again the words of the text. "As by learning the alphabets one can, through practice, master all the sciences, so by thoroughly practising first the (physical) training, one acquires the Knowledge of the True." The training I have here communicated faithfully; but the

---

42) *Siva Samhita*, v, 210–12. A similar comment is made in another section, 185–7. "Let him practise this in secrecy, free from the company of men, in a retired place. For the sake of appearance he should remain in society, but should not have his heart in it. He should not renounce the duties of his profession, caste or rank; but let him perform these merely as an instrument of the Lord, without any thought of the event. By thus doing there is no sin. Even the householder (Grihastha) by wisely following this method may obtain success, there is no doubt of it. Remaining in the midst of the family, always doing the duties of the householder, he who is free from merits and demerits, and has restrained his senses, attains salvation. The householder practising Yoga is not touched by sins, if to protect mankind he does any sin, he is not polluted by it."

43) *Siva Samhita*, v, 207. Compare *Hatha Yoga Pradipika*, i, II; for description see p. 17.

"Knowledge of the True," because of its very nature, must remain a mystery.

THE END

LIST OF ILLUSTRATIONS

— Ardha Padmasana (lotus posture) —

— [I] Sarvangasana (shoulder stand) —

— [II] Matsyasana (fish posture) —

— [III] Halasana (plough posture) —

— [IV] Halasana (fully extended) —

— [V] Halasana (another variation) —

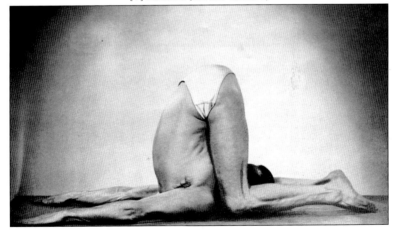

— [VI] Pascimottanasana (posterior stretching posture) —

— [VII] Maha Mudra —

— [VIII] Mayurasana (peacock posture) —

— [IX] Mayurasana (another variation) —

— [X] Salabhasana (locust posture) —

— [XI] Bhujangasana (cobra posture) —

— [XII] Dhanurasana (bow posture) —

— [XIII] Ardha Matsyendrasana (half spine twist) —

— [XIV] Matsyendrasana (completed spine twist) —

— [XV] Siddhasana with Jalandhara and Uddiyana Bandha —
(accomplished posture, with chin lock)

— [XVI] Vajrasana (thunderbolt posture) —

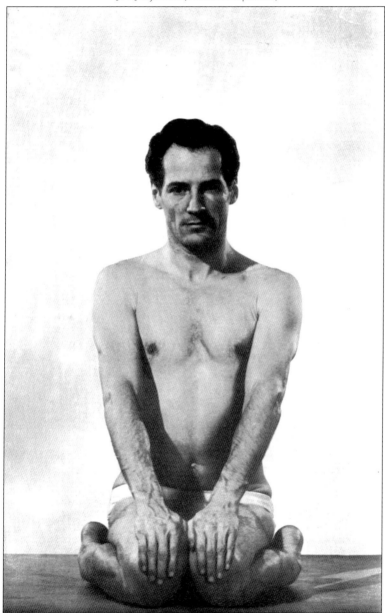

— [XVII] Supta Vajrasana (supine thunderbolt posture) —

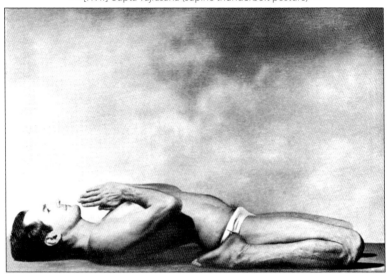

— [XVIII] Vajrasana (another variation) —

— [XIX] Samkatasana (dangerous posture) —

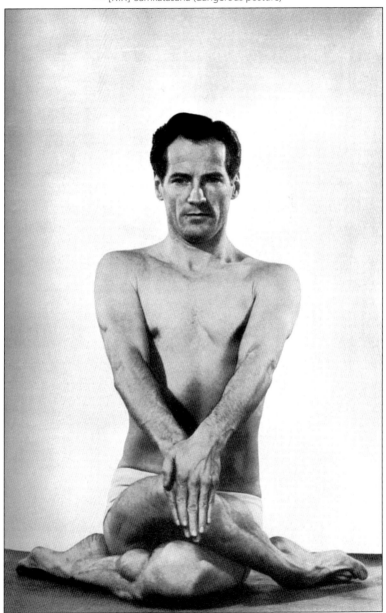

— [XX] Baddha Padmasana (locked lotus posture) —

— [XXI] Padmasana (another variation) —

— [XXII] Virasana (hero posture) —

— [XXIII] Kukkutasana (cock posture) —

— [XXIV] Uttanakurmakasana (stretched like tortoise posture)—

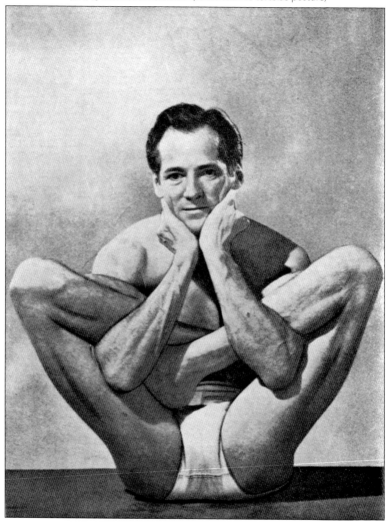

— [XXV] Yogasana —

— [XXVI] Vajroli Mudra —

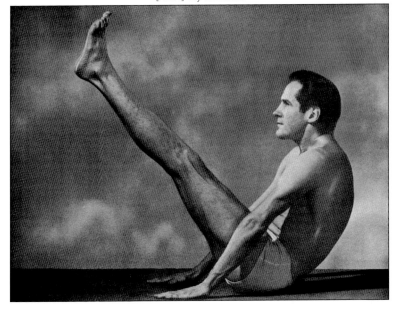

— [XXVII] Pasini Mudra (noose mudra) —

— [XXVIII] Sirsasana (head stand in padmasana) —

— [XXIX] Sirsasana (head stand, with legs lowered) —

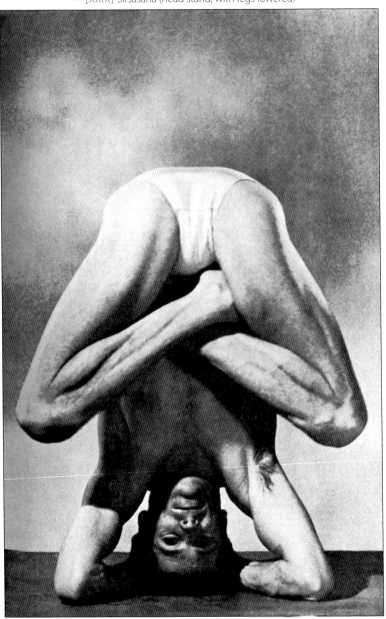

— [XXX] Vrksasana (tree posture) —

— [XXXI] Padhahasthasana —

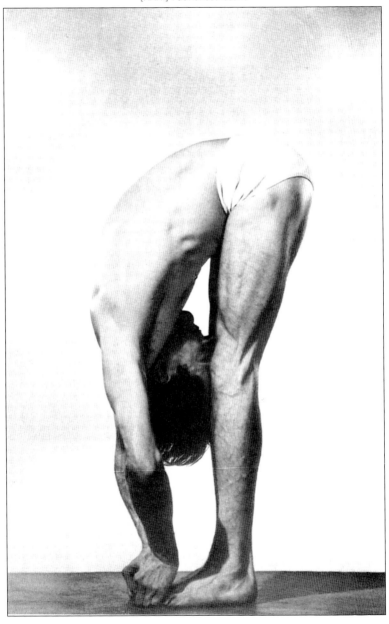

— [XXXII] Uddiyana Bandha (first stage) —

— [XXXIII] Uddiyana Bandha (second stage) —

— [XXXIV] Nauli Madhyama (central aspect of nauli) —

— [XXXV] Nauli Vama (left aspect of nauli) —

— [XXXVI] Nauli Dakshina (right aspect of nauli) —

About the Author

The story of Theos Bernard begins in the deserts of southern Arizona. Raised by his mother in Tombstone, Bernard entered the newly founded University of Arizona, in Tucson, in 1928. Bernard's early college years were interrupted, however, by a near fatal illness which profoundly altered his life. It was while convalescing in the Dragoon Mountains that Bernard met his first spiritual teacher, a yogi from India who had been a friend of his family for many years, who began to instruct him in the fundamentals of yoga. Although he had been pursuing a degree in law, Bernard completed his studies in 1934 only to turn to religious and philosophical pursuits.

Theos Bernard entered Columbia University in the fall of 1934, immediately following his graduation from the University of Arizona. At the time of his entry, there was no formal program of studies in religion, and courses on the subject had only been being taught for seven years, mostly through the efforts of Bernard's advisor in the philosophy department, Herbert Schneider. The records of Bernard's career during this time are sparse, and his official transcript gives no account of any classes taken or grades received, noting only that on June 2, 1936, he was awarded the degree of Masters of Arts (AM).

Of his own account, though Bernard's first two publications are autobiographical and tell the story of his education and pursuit of authentic religious instruction, they give no account of his years at Columbia. Rather, Heaven Lies Within Us and Penthouse of the Gods were both published following his trips to India and Tibet from 1936–37 and textually laid the groundwork for his later books through the narrative of a personally validated authentic religious tradition. The full context of Bernard's life story lies unspoken in the world of his uncle, Pierre Bernard, and New York's high society of the 1920s and 1930s.

Pierre Bernard (aka Oom the Omnipotent) founded the New York Sanskrit College in midtown Manhattan in the early part of the twentieth century. Together with his wife, Blanche de Vries, Oom began instructing a number of wealthy New York socialites in the science and practices of yoga. Chief among Oom's students was Mrs. Vanderbilt, who funneled not only friends, but a substantial amount of money his way to establish a discreet sanctuary in which Oom could lecture and instruct. The result was The Mystic Order of the Tantriks of India and an estate that was to become the Clarkstown Country Club in Nyack, New York. Here Oom did, indeed, lecture and instruct on the practices of yoga–even publishing a journal–but also provided a socially liberal yet exclusive resort for young New Yorkers, and put at their disposal a world-class research library described as "approximately

7,000 volumes on the subjects of philosophy, ethics, psychology, education and metaphysics as well as much collateral material on physiology, medicine and the related sciences." More significantly however, Oom provided his services—either directly or incidentally—as a matchmaker for the membership. It was into this world that he brought his nephew, Theos Bernard, who eventually married a niece of Henry Morgenthau Sr., Viola Wertheim.

"I had become aware of my discovery of those deep joys that I had never before dreampt existed in this life, and I felt that all my effort gained for me a reward altogether overwhelming"

INDIA AND TIBET

Completing his master's degree in 1936, and with the financial leisure accorded him by his marriage, Bernard was able to embark on an extensive trip to India and Tibet in late summer of 1936. Narrating his account, Bernard tells of seeking out the teacher of Hindu yogi whom he had met once in Arizona through his mother. Arriving in India in time only to hear of the death of his would-be guru, Bernard sought out other teachers in India traveling the length and breadth of the country, from Kasmir to Ceylon (Sri Lanka) taking religious initiations and instruction on various yogic techniques. He finally made his way to Calcutta where he was able to make contacts which eventually led to a meeting with and becoming a student of Lama Tharchin in Kalimpong. Here, Bernard spent a period of intensive study of the Tibetan written language and three spoken dialects. After close to a year in India, he was finally able to secure permission from the British political officer in Sikkim, J. B. Gould to travel to Tibet. Once there, Bernard had audiences with the Ganden Tri-pa, the Regent of Tibet, Reting Rinpoche, and numerous other officials in the Tibetan government. In addition, Bernard received Tantric empowerments, engaged in a meditative retreat, and acquired numerous books included a complete set of the Buddhist canon, a set of the Treasury of Revealed Teachings (rin chen gter mdzod) and several hundred more volumes of Tibetan works.

Shortly after returning from India and Tibet, Theos Bernard was divorced by his wife Viola. Completing his first two books, Bernard began touring, giving a series of lectures in America and Europe. Promoting himself and his new books in England, Bernard authored several magazine articles both about the political situation in Tibet and his experiences there. In conjunction with the British publication of Penthouse of the Gods (published under the title of Land of a Thousand Buddhas), Bernard's accounts were picked up by the British tabloid press at the time, and, though their sensationalistic reports concerning his identity as "a white Lama" garnered some positive public feedback and interest, it also earned him the scorn and private dismissal of British Intelligence operatives (who had monitored his activities since his first entry into Tibet) as a fraud and imposter.

In the West, there is the preconceived notion that man cannot know metaphysical truths by direct experience; therefore, at best, metaphysical truths can only be speculations, inferences, or ungrounded faith.

Returning to America, Bernard continued working on his dissertation at Columbia University, Hatha Yoga: The Report of a Personal Experience (1943). He began teaching and lecturing on yoga on the Upper East side of Manhattan, where he met a wealthy Polish opera star who first became one of his students and, later, a romantic interest. Within a year, Bernard and Ganna Walska were married and the two moved to California where they purchased a large piece of land, which they named Tibetland to house Bernard's collection of Tibetan manuscripts, provide accommodations for visiting Tibetan lamas, and to serve as the center for his translation efforts. Bernard's marriage to Ganna Walska was short lived, however. While Walska proceeded to convert the property into a horticultural museum (Lotusland), Bernard produced a fourth book, The Philosophical Foundations of India, and together with his third wife, Helen, returned to India in 1947, this time seeking "rare manuscripts" in the hills of Spiti near Ladakh. Entering the Punjab en route to his destination, his party of Muslim porters was rumored to have been attacked by Lahouli tribesman. Conflicting reports about his whereabouts circulated for several months, and though his wife waited for him in Calcutta, he never returned. Despite his talents and good fortunes which had led him so far, in the end Bernard never saw his aspirations fulfilled and, like Tibet, fell victim to the larger forces at play during the twilight of the old empires.

RECOMMENDED READING

PRIMARY SOURCES

Rama-Prasada, tr., *Patanjali's Yoga Sutras with the commentary of Vyasa and the Gloss of Vachaspati Misra.* 3rd ed. Allahabad, Pub. by Sudhindranath Vasu, The Panini Office, 1924. Sacred Books of the Hindus, Vol. IV.

Sinh, Pancham, tr., *Hatha Yoga Pradipika.* 2nd ed. Allahabad, Pub. by Lalit Mohan Basu, The Panini Office, 1932.

Vidyarnava. Rai Bahadur Srisa Chandra, tr., *Siva Samhita.* 2nd ed. Allahabad, Pub. by Sudhindra Nath Basu, The Panini Office, 1923.

Vasu, Sris Chandra, tr., *Gheranda Samhita.* Adyar, Madras, Theosophical Publishing House, 1933.

Woods, James Haughton, tr., *The Yoga-System of Patanjali.* Cambridge, Mass., The Harvard University Press, 1914. Harvard Oriental Series, Vol. XVII.

SECONDARY SOURCES

Attreya, B. L., *The Philosophy of the Yoga-Vasistha.* Adyar, Madras, Theosophical Publishing House, 1936.

Avalon, Arthur, *Principles of Tantra.* Parts I and II; ed. with introduction and commentary. London, Luzac and Co., 1914, 1916.

— *Serpent Power*; tr. with introduction and commentary. Madras, Ganesh and Co., 1924.

— tr., *The Great Liberation*; tr. with commentary. Madras, Ganesh and Co., 1927.

Behanan, Kovoor T., *Yoga; a Scientific Evaluation.* New York, Macmillan Company, 1938.

Bhishagratna, Kaviraj Kunga Lal, ed., *Sushruta Samhita.* 3 vols. Calcutta, Bharat Mihir Press, 1907, 1911, 1916.

Briggs, G. W., *Gorakhnath and the Kanphata Yogis.* London, Oxford University Press, 1938.

Dasgupta, Surendra Nath, *Yoga as Philosophy and Religion*. London, Kegan Paul, Trench, Truber and Co., Ltd., 1924.

— *Yoga Philosophy in Relation to Other Systems of Indian Thought*. Calcutta, University of Calcutta, 1930.

Demaitre, Edmond, *The Yogis of India*. London, G. Blas. 1937.

Evans-Wentz, W. Y., ed.. *The Tibetan Book of the Dead*. London, Oxford University Press, 1927.

—*Tibetan Yoga and Secret Doctrines*. London, Oxford University Press, 1935.

—*Tibet's Great Yogi Milarepa*. London, Oxford University Press, 1928.

Flagg, William J., *Yoga or Transformation*. New York, J.W. Bouton; London; G. Redway, 1898.

Garbe, Richard von, *Samkhya und Yoga*. Strassburg, K. J. Trübner, 1896.

Ghosh, Janeswar, *A Study of Yoga*. Calcutta, Emerald Printing Works, 1933.

Jha, Ganganatha, tr., *Yoga Darsana*. Bombay, Rajaram Tukaram Tatya, 1907.

—*Yogasara-Sangraha of Vijnana Bhikshu*. Bombay, Tatva-Vivechaka Press, 1894.

Kavirtna, Kaviraj Avinash Chandra, tr., *Charaka Samhita*. Calcutta, 200 Cornwallis St., Published by author, 1890. 4 vols.

Kuvalayananda, Srimat Asanas. Bombay, Kaivalyadhama, Lonavla, 1933.

—*Pranayama*. Bombay, Kaivalyadhama, Lonavla, 1931.

— *Yoga Mimansa Journals*. Bombay, Kaivalydahama, Lonavla. First published in 1924; now discontinued.

Mitra, Vihari Lala, tr., *The Yoga-Vasishtha Maharamayana of Valmiki*. Calcutta, Kahinoor Press, 1893. 4 vols.

Narayanaswami Aiyar, K., tr., *Yoga Vasistha*. Madras, K. N. Aiyar, 1914.

Oman, John Campbell, *The Mystics, Ascetics, and Saints of India*. London, Unwin, 1903

Paul, M. C., *A Treatise on the Yoga Philosophy*. Bombay, Tatva-Vivechaka Press, 1899.

Rele, V. G., *The Mysterious Kundalini*. Bombay, D. B. Taraporevala Sons and Co., 1927.

Rele, V. G., *Yogic Asanas*. Bombay, D. B. Taraporevala Sons and Co., 1939.

Roy, A. T., *Nervous System of the Ancient Hindu*. Hazaribagh, 1930.

Sastri, S. S. Suryanarayana, tr., *Samkhya Karika of Isvarakrsna* Madras, University of Madras, 1930.

Schmidt, Richard, *Fakire und Fakirtum im alten und modernen Indien*. Berlin, von Hermann Barsdorf, 1908.

Singh, Mohan, *Gorakhnatha and Mediaeval Hindu Mysticism*. Lahore, Oriental College, 1937.

Sundaram, S., *Yogic Physical Culture*. Bangalore, The Brahmacharya Publishing House, 1931.

Vithaldas, Yogi, *The Yoga System of Health*. London, Faber and Faber, Ltd., 1939.

Woodroffe, Sir John, *Shakti and Shakta*. Madras, Ganesh and Co., 1929.

—*The Garland of Letters*. Madras, Ganesh and Co., 1922.

Yogendra, Shri, *Yoga Personal Hygiene*. Bombay, The Yoga Institute, 1940.

INDEX